Advance Praise

Who's Watching the

Improving the Quality of Family, Frien

I0789374

"This extremely valuable book by an outstanding scholar illuminates the most underexplored issue in the provision of child care to America's children."
—Edward Zigler, Sterling Professor of Psychology, Emeritus, and
 Director, Emeritus, Edward Zigler Center, Yale University

"Finally, there is a book that synthesizes and analyzes the best research on reaching out to, working with, and improving the quality of family, friend, and neighbor care. Written with uncommon wisdom and brilliant insight, this book is a true treasure!"
—Ellen Galinsky, President and Co-Founder, Families and Work Institute,
 New York City

"THE most lucid thoughtful analysis of FFN to date!! Powell's work gives voice to this too often neglected and critically important component of early education. The book pierces the polemics, distinctions, and issues to render an absolutely essential read for all who care about the future of young children."
—Sharon Lynn Kagan, Virginia and Leonard Marx Professor of Early Childhood
 and Family Policy, Teachers College, Columbia University

"This book makes an extremely valuable contribution, summarizing in a clear and accessible way the emerging body of research on how to reach and support the family, friends and neighbors who are providing child care to so many of our infants and toddlers. The book reflects a deep understanding of the challenges involved in identifying strategies to improve the quality of this care while respecting the special nature of the relationships between family, friend and neighbor care-giveres and the families they are providing care for."
—Martha Zaslow, Vice President for Research and Senior Scholar, Child Trends,
 Washington, DC

"This book makes a major contribution toward better research in FFN early child care. Not only does Powell point out the complexity of such research, but challenges researchers to examine and measure more appropriate variables, such as cultural continuity and interpersonal relationships in FFN care by family, race, or ethnicity."
—Dolores Norton, Samuel Deutsch Professor, School of Social Service
 Administration, The University of Chicago

The Irving B. Harris Award
of the ZERO TO THREE Press

Douglas R. Powell is the winner of an Irving B. Harris Award of the ZERO TO THREE Press. Created by the late Irving B. Harris, these generous stipends offered essential support to outstanding authors for the development of book manuscripts that address issues of emerging importance to the multi-disciplinary infant–family field. The ZERO TO THREE Press Editorial Board selected the recipients from among manuscripts submitted for consideration during five competitions. *Who's Watching the Babies?: Improving the Quality of Family, Friend, and Neighbor Care* is a result of Harris' generosity and belief in the power of books to make a lasting difference in the way we care for infants, toddlers, and families.

Who's Watching the Babies?

Improving the Quality of Family, Friend, and Neighbor Care

Douglas R. Powell

ZERO
TO
THREE®

National Center for Infants, Toddlers, and Families

Washington, DC

Published by

ZERO TO THREE
2000 M St., NW, Suite 200
Washington, DC 20036-3307
(202) 638-1144
Toll-free orders (800) 899-4301
Fax: (202) 638-0851
Web: http://www.zerotothree.org

The mission of the ZERO TO THREE Press is to publish authoritative research, practical resources, and new ideas for those who work with and care about infants, toddlers, and their families. Books are selected for publication by an independent Editorial Board.

The views contained in this book are those of the authors and do not necessarily reflect those of ZERO TO THREE: National Center for Infants, Toddlers and Families, Inc.

These materials are intended for education and training to help promote a high standard of care by professionals. Use of these materials is voluntary and their use does not confer any professional credentials or qualification to take any registration, certification, board or licensure examination, and neither confers nor infers competency to perform any related professional functions.

The user of these materials is solely responsible for compliance with all local, state or federal rules, regulations or licensing requirements. Despite efforts to ensure that these materials are consistent with acceptable practices, they are not intended to be used as a compliance guide and are not intended to supplant or to be used as a substitute for or in contravention of any applicable local, state or federal rules, regulations or licensing requirements. ZERO TO THREE expressly disclaims any liability arising from use of these materials in contravention of such rules, regulations or licensing requirements.

The views expressed in these materials represent the opinions of the respective authors. Publication of these materials does not constitute an endorsement by ZERO TO THREE of any view expressed herein, and ZERO TO THREE expressly disclaims any liability arising from any inaccuracy or misstatement.

Cover and text design and composition: K Art and Design, Inc.

Library of Congress Cataloging-in-Publication Data

Powell, Douglas R.
      Who's watching the babies? : improving the quality of family, friend, and neighbor care / Douglas R. Powell.
            p.   cm.
      ISBN 978-1-934019-21-4
            1. Child care--United States. 2. Family day care--United States. 3. Child care services--United States. I. Title.
      HQ778.63.P68 2008
      362.71'2--dc22
                                                                                    2007039263

For permission for academic photocopying (for course packets, study materials, etc.) by copy centers, educators, or university bookstores or libraries, of this and other ZERO TO THREE materials, please contact Copyright Clearance Center, 222 Rosewood Drive, Danvers, MA 01923; phone, (978) 750-8400; fax, (978) 750-4744; or visit its Web site at www.copyright.com.

ISBN 978-1-934019-21-4

Printed in the United States of America

10 9 8 7 6 5 4 3 2 1

Suggested citation: Powell, D. R. (2008). *Who's watching the babies? Improving the quality of family, friend, and neighbor care*. Washington, DC: ZERO TO THREE.

In memory of my grandmother,
Bessie J. Van Siclen Warner

Table of Contents

Foreword

*F*amily, friend, and neighbor (FFN) care is a vital sector of the broader early care and education field in this country. Yet policy makers, researchers, and administrators face almost insurmountable challenges in recruiting FFN providers and presenting them with information and resources focused on ensuring a safe, appropriate early learning experience for the almost 50% of children under the age of 5 years who are served in FFN care. The Child Care Bureau, whose mission is to support low-income working families, has noted the paucity of research on FFN and the need for effective professional development models and policies for providers who are outside the regulatory system in many states. The Child Care Bureau also states that many of of those families express a preference for FFN care over formal child care arrangements (Child Care Bureau, 2007). Despite the recognition that FFN providers are integral to the child care workforce and the need to make high quality FFN care available and accessible to all families who need it, until now, reliable information on this important topic has been difficult to find.

Finally, in response to the need for the best available research on these issues combined with the field's collective wisdom and values, Powell offers us a valuable resource: *Who's Watching the Babies: Improving the Quality of Family, Friend, and Neighbor Care.* Beginning with a proposed definition of FFN, this volume presents key characteristics of the often "invisible" relatives, friends, and community members who care for young children in this country and connects the needs and priorities of FFN providers with promising practices for supporting and enhancing the quality of FFN.

Throughout the book, Powell presents the reader with an impressive synthesis of the "thin" research on FFN care, and perhaps more important, an honest appraisal of what these findings mean for the early childhood field. For example, he questions whether conventional ways of defining child outcomes and measuring the effects of child care translate to contexts in which children may be related to their caregivers and in which racial and ethnic identity are considered an important benefit of those FFN arrangements. The research synthesis on FFN presented in this volume should spark future interest and inquiry on a wide range of topics related to FFN care: the characteristics of the providers, along with effective approaches for supporting these providers and enhancing the quality of FFN care; the characteristics and priorities of the children and families served; and the perceived and observed outcomes of FFN care.

Perhaps the most valuable contribution that Powell offers is a summary of existing models and initiatives that respond to the needs of the FFN community. The description of these approaches is organized to address three questions: (1) How do programs and their host agencies prepare to work with FFN providers, (2) what are effective ways to find and engage FFN providers, and (3) what methods are useful in responding to the needs of FFN providers? In answering these questions, Powell offers the field insightful observations that remind us that initiatives aimed at creating effective professional development programs and strategies for enhancing the quality of FFN must begin with a thorough understanding of who experiences FFN care, what their needs and priorities are, and the potential of FFN care to enhance early development and family support for young children and families everywhere.

Reference

Child Care Bureau. (2007, Fall). *Child Care Bulletin*, Issue 34.

Virginia Buysse
FPG Child Development Institute
University of North Carolina at Chapel Hill

Acknowledgments

This volume is an outgrowth of my participation in the Archibald Bush Foundation's child development grant-making area. I am indebted to Jane Kretzmann, senior program officer, for her vision of and spirited commitment to a better world for infants and toddlers. Bush consultant Mary Kay Stranik provided respectful support to the initiative described in chapter 5. Her thoughtful perspectives on the work enriched my understanding of community-based program development processes. I learned immeasurably from the staff and caregivers who participated in the Bush effort. Preparation of this book benefited from the encouragement of the late Emily Fenichel as well as her editorial advice on drafts of the first two chapters. I am thankful to ZERO TO THREE Press for the Harris award and the opportunity to contribute this volume to the field.

Chapter 1

Characteristics and Quality of Family, Friend, and Neighbor Child Care

Societal interest in ensuring that very young children get off to a good start in life is at an exceptionally high level. A growing body of impressive research findings points to the long-term consequences of the quality of children's early experiences with parents and other caregivers and to the numerous benefits of responsive care environments. In both public and private sectors, there is a renewed commitment to finding innovative ways to provide an enduring foundation of support for optimal child development in the earliest years of life.

One of the promising pathways to improving children's developmental outcomes is to provide education, training, and related resources to individuals in parenting roles and to staff in programs of early education and care. Since the 1980s, there has been significant growth in the number and type of programs aimed at bolstering the knowledge and skills of adults who care for young children. The efforts include family support programs, parenting education, and training and professional development initiatives for staff in a range of early childhood settings.

Among the most challenging populations for programs to reach is the largely invisible set of persons who care for infants and toddlers through informal arrangements with families. For generations, parents have entrusted the care of their young children to family members, friends, and neighbors (FFN). Today this highly diverse group of persons makes a substantial contribution to the nation's child care needs. It also is a group with limited access to conventional resources for supporting optimal child outcomes, including early school success.

Early childhood professional development initiatives are generally ill equipped to connect with most caregivers in informal settings (Kreader & Lawrence, 2006). Child care resource and referral agencies in one state, for example, found that including educational opportunities for informal caregivers in widely distributed catalog schedules of child care provider training sessions yielded few if any participants who provide care through informal arrangements (Myers, n.d.).

FFN providers who regularly care for infants and toddlers are poorly understood. They are often described by what they are *not*: they are not legally licensed, not trained, and not connected to formal systems of education and support. The stereotypical portrayals run the risk of masking a more nuanced understanding of the needs and interests of FFN caregivers.

Long overlooked, the informal sector of early education and care is increasingly difficult to ignore. Estimates indicate that approximately 1.1 million providers—about one half of the paid early care and education workforce—care for children birth to 5 years of age in informal settings. This group includes paid relatives (35% or 804,000) and paid nonrelatives (13% or 298,000). In addition, an estimated 650,000 members (28%) of the paid early childhood workforce are family child care providers, some of whom may legally operate unlicensed family child care homes. These numbers are particularly impressive in comparison to the approximately 3.5 million teachers in public and private K–12 schools (Brandon & Martinez-Beck, 2006) and do not include relatives, friends, and neighbors who regularly care for young children without pay.

In addition to sheer numbers, informal caregivers deserve thoughtful attention because they are the largest nonparental source of child care for infants and toddlers. Renewed attention to the importance of the early years, coupled with research on caregiver competence as an indicator of child care quality, have led to increases in staff development activities as pathways to improvements in early childhood environments (Zaslow & Martinez-Beck, 2006). Yet improvements in the availability and effectiveness of valuable forms of professional development are unlikely to impact the vast majority of "staff" who care for infants and toddlers as part of their role as grandmother, aunt, and family friend in the neighborhood.

The prevalence of informal care settings also is difficult to ignore because lower income parents can now use public child care subsidies, previously limited to licensed facilities, to purchase child care from relatives and other informal providers. This provision is part of the Personal Responsibility and Work Opportunity Reconciliation Act of 1996, which also significantly increased the need for child care by placing more stringent work requirements on parents, including parents of very young children (Greenberg et al., 2001). The use of public funds for informal caregivers is controversial among early childhood professionals, some of whom view the provision as contributing to an erosion of standards for quality (e.g., Gordon, 2000).

This volume provides a guide to developing and implementing programs of support designed to promote high quality in the care of infants and toddlers by FFN caregivers. The book is organized around major decisions in the program development and implementation process, which are outlined at the end of this chapter. The remainder of this chapter provides a summary of what we know about the characteristics and quality of informal care settings.

Characteristics

Child care provided by FFN is defined differently across states, other government entities, and studies. This makes it difficult to make comparisons across initiatives aimed at supporting FFN child care and across different studies. One point of difference in definitions is whether nonrelative care in the provider's unlicensed home is defined as family child care or as FFN child care (Susman-Stillman, 2005). Another point of difference is the extent to which the definition includes more than subsidized care. Some views of FFN care focus largely or exclusively on subsidized settings that are legally unlicensed or unregistered. This subset of the FFN population is a useful place to begin in designing and implementing strategies to support informal settings, but it does not represent the full range of FFN child care arrangements.

For this volume, FFN child care providers include relatives and non-relatives who are not licensed or regulated by a government agency for the provision of child care. This includes family members, friends, neighbors, nannies, and individuals sometimes called "babysitters." This type of child care is sometimes called *kith and kin, informal care, legally unlicensed*, or *license-exempt* care. Care may be provided in the caregiver's home or in the child's home.

The Scope of Family, Friend, and Neighbor Care

- Family, friend, and neighbor (FFN) caregivers are the most common source of nonparental care of infants and toddlers, and they often provide care in combination with other arrangements for preschool-age and school-age children. Grandparents are major providers of FFN child care.

- All types of families use FFN child care. Relative care is slightly more common among lower income than higher income families. African American children compared to other populations are more likely to be cared for by a relative.

- Parents use FFN child care for many reasons, including knowing and trusting the caregiver, flexible hours, and accommodation of nonstandard work hours. Some parents use FFN care out of necessity rather than preference.

Extent of FFN Child Care

The extent to which infants and toddlers are regularly in the care of nonparental relatives, friends, and neighbors is demonstrated in recent statistics from the U.S. Census Bureau. Information from the Census Bureau's 2002 Survey of Income and Program Participation regarding employed mothers' child care arrangements indicates that infants and toddlers are cared for at least once a week by the following:

- Grandparents: 34% of infants (under 1 year of age), 30% of toddlers (1–2 years of age)

- Other nonparental relatives: 10% of infants, 11% of toddlers

- Nonrelatives in child's home: 3% of infants, 6% of toddlers

- Other nonrelatives in provider's home (likely includes friends or neighbors who are not licensed as family child care providers): 6% of infants, 6% of toddlers

- Family child care homes: 11% of infants, 11% of toddlers

- Center-based programs: 16% of infants, 25% of toddlers (Johnson, 2005; see Figure 1.1).

About 17% of infants and toddlers of mothers who are in school and/or do not work outside of the home also are cared for at least once a week by a grandparent (Johnson, 2005).

Results of other national surveys also point to the significant role of relatives and other informal providers in the care of infants and toddlers. Notable data sources include the National Education Household Survey and the Early Childhood Longitudinal Survey, Birth Cohort, both conducted by the National Center for Education Statistics (http://nces.ed.gov), and the National Survey of America's Families conducted by the Urban Institute (www.urban.org). In addition, recent child care surveys in the states of Illinois (Anderson, Ramsburg, & Scott, 2005), Minnesota (Chase, Arnold, Schauben, & Shardlow, 2005), and Washington (Brandon, Maher, Joesch, & Doyle, 2002) show that FFN caregivers are the most common nonparental source of care for infants and toddlers.

Relatives—particularly grandparents—are the most common source of informal child care, as indicated above. More is known about the use of relative care than other forms of FFN care, partly because relative care is easier to identify in surveys (e.g., parents may not know whether a family child care provider is licensed).

Approximately 37% of children under 3 years of age whose parents were employed spent 35 or more hours a week in the care of a relative.

Fig. 1.1: Child Care for Infants and Toddlers of Employed Mothers

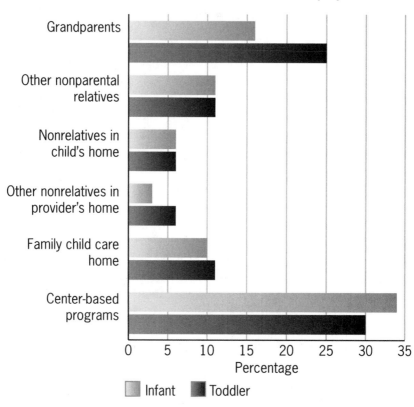

Source: Johnson, 2005

The percentage of children in relative care 35 or more hours a week dropped to 31% for children 3 to 4 years old. This information comes from the 1999 National Survey of America's Families (Snyder & Adelman, 2004). As children grow older, they are more likely to be in center-based programs. When the 2002 U.S. Census information was collected, 16% of children less than 1 year old were in a child care center compared to sizeable percentages of children 3 to 4 years old who were in centers (25%), nursery and preschool programs (14%), or Head Start programs (12%; Johnson, 2005).

Relative care is the *only* arrangement for higher percentages of children less than 3 years old than for any other age group (Snyder & Adelman, 2004). Small percentages of children less than 3 years old are cared for by relatives in combination with other arrangements (about 6% in 1999 and 7% in 2001; Snyder, Dore, & Adelman, 2005). Information from the

Early Childhood Longitudinal Study, Birth Cohort, indicates that children in relative care at age 9 months were more likely to be in care for 10 or fewer hours a week than children in nonrelative (in-home or family child care) or center care (Kreader, Ferguson, & Lawrence, 2005).

Even though the number of children in center-based programs increases with child age, relative care continues to be a component of many child care arrangements across different stages of childhood. Children who are 3 and 4 years old are more likely than other age groups to be in relative care as part of a combination of nonparental child care arrangements, and almost one in five 3- and 4-year-old children are in relative care only when their parents are at work. One quarter of children 6- to 12-years-old spend some time in relative care while their parents work (Snyder & Adelman, 2004).

Nonparental care of children less than 6 years old is more likely to be provided in a home other than the child's regardless of whether the care is provided by a relative or nonrelative. In the 2001 National Education Household Survey, the child care arrangements of 66% of children receiving care from their relatives, for example, were located in homes other than their own (Mulligan, Brimhall, West, & Chapman, 2005).

In general, child care arrangements appear to be quite fluid. A large prospective study of child care arrangements found that children did not fit into clear patterns of care over time. Fewer than 20% of children who received nonmaternal care stayed in the same type of care from 6 to 54 months old, and only 17% moved "cleanly" from informal to more formal care at or after age 3 years. Some children would leave care entirely for periods of time or switch from informal to formal and back to informal care at different age points (NICHD Early Child Care Research Network, 2004, p. 224).

Who Uses FFN Child Care and Why

All types of families with young children use FFN child care. There were no significant household income differences in the use of relative child care in analyses of information collected in 1995 (Early & Burchinal, 2001) and in 2001 (Mulligan et al., 2005) by the National

Household Education Survey. However, the 2002 National Survey of America's Families found that about 32% of low-income infants and toddlers were in relative care on a regular basis (at least once a week) compared to about 26% of infants and toddlers from higher income families (Capizzano & Adams, 2003).

Although the use of FFN child care cuts across different social groups, there are some differences in the use of relatives and nonrelative child care arrangements by family race and/or ethnicity background and by maternal education levels. In the 2001 National Household Education Survey, African American infants were more likely than White infants to receive care from a relative (31% vs. 18%), and White infants were more likely than Hispanic infants to receive care from a nonrelative (17% vs. 7%). With regard to 2-year-old children, African American toddlers were more likely than White or Hispanic toddlers to be cared for by a relative (31% vs. 20% and 22%, respectively; Mulligan et al., 2005). These patterns are similar to results of the 1995 National Household Education Survey regardless of poverty status (Early & Burchinal, 2001). Among infants, 2001 national survey information indicated that participation in relative care arrangements was more common when mothers had a high school diploma or equivalent, a vocational or technical diploma, or some college (25%–27%) than when mothers had less than a high school education (14%) or a bachelor's degree or higher (15%). Among toddlers, participation in nonrelative and center-based care increased as maternal education increased (Mulligan et al., 2005).

Parents use FFN child care for many reasons. Some parents trust and prefer care by relatives over other child care possibilities. In one study of working-class families in a small city in the Northeast, for example, mothers trusted their own mothers more than anyone else to provide good care for their babies (Zinsser, 1991). Parents relied on grandmothers and other close relatives as "repositories of family values, traditions, and sometimes language" (Zinsser, 2001, p. 124). There are suggestions that parents may prefer that their very young children be in the care of individuals who represent the same cultural or racial and/or ethnic background (Brandon & Martinez-Beck, 2006; Emerita, 2006). Relative and family child care providers are typically the same racial and ethnic background of the children in their care (Kontos, Howes, Shinn, &

Galinsky, 1995), but the extent to which this is a function of the racial and ethnic composition of family social networks or strong parental values regarding cultural continuity in child rearing is not clear. Studies consistently indicate that knowing and trusting the caregiver, attention to the child's safety and cleanliness, and the caregiver's warmth and attention to the child are highly important to parents of very young children (e.g., Pungello & Kurtz-Costes, 1999). These factors may prompt parents to avoid centers for their babies and toddlers, but they may not be unique to parents who use FFN child care. One study found no major differences in definitions of child care quality across parents using regulated family child care, unregulated family child care, and relative care (Kontos et al., 1995).

Concerns about possible negative effects of maternal employment on young children may shape some mothers' decisions to use FFN care. In a study of patterns of nonmaternal child care during the first 15 months of a child's life, mothers who thought employment had high risks were more likely than others to use shared parental or grandparent care. Mothers who thought employment had relatively low risks for their child were more likely to use formal care in family child care homes or centers (NICHD Early Child Care Research Network, 1997).

Flexible hours and the provision of care during evening hours appear to be influences on some parents' decisions to use of FFN child care. In one study, for example, relative care was the most common form of care for children under 3 years of age among nonmarried mothers who worked nonstandard hours (Han, 2004). The lower cost of FFN child care may be another appealing factor. Nearly one half of relatives in one multisite study did not charge for care (Galinsky, Howes, Kontos, & Shinn, 1994).

Parents may use FFN care out of necessity rather than preference. A longitudinal ethnographic study of welfare-to-work transitions of families in Cleveland, Ohio, and Philadelphia, Pennsylvania, found that some mothers reluctantly used relatives—including relatives who were reportedly neglectful or punitive—because they could not afford or access other forms of care (Clampet-Lundquist, Edin, London, Scott, & Hunter, 2004). Research on the child-care arrangements of poor families found that city of residence was a more powerful predictor of the quality of child care selected by parents than maternal and family factors. These results suggest there is wide variation in the capacity of states or local communities to widen poor families' access to higher quality child care (Fuller, Kagan, Loeb, & Chang, 2004).

Regional differences in the use of FFN care raise interesting and unanswered questions about parent choices, including the availability of accessible options. For example, infants who live in the Northeast are more likely to be cared for by relatives than infants living in the South or the West (28% vs. 19% in each), whereas infants in the Midwest are more likely than infants in the South and West to have nonrelative child care arrangements (20% vs. 11% and 12%, respectively; Mulligan et al., 2005).

Quality

Generalizations about FFN child care reflect a full range of views, from portrayals of informal care settings as harmful influences on children's well-being to images of FFN care arrangements as uniquely resourceful systems of support for very young children and their parents. Fortunately, results of a growing set of child care studies enable us to draw on more than idiosyncratic impressions or anecdotes for answers to critically important questions about the quality and consequences of FFN child care.

Assessing What We Know

Studies of child care quality and effects are among the most complicated of all scientific endeavors. Researchers have made significant progress in some areas and continue to grapple with challenges in other areas.

One of the recent advances in child care research is the inclusion of a broad range of child care types. Child care centers and family child care homes have long been the primary or sole focus of child care research. FFN arrangements are increasingly among the types of child care examined in studies of child care quality. Researchers also are giving more careful attention to the possibility that the effects of different types or quality of child care settings may be explained by preexisting family

The State of Research on Family, Friend, and Neighbor Child Care

- Existing research information is limited. Informal settings of child care have been studied far less than formal settings. Family, friend, and neighbor (FFN) child care is often defined differently across studies and child care samples are not representative.

- A major research issue is the appropriateness of commonly used measures of child care quality for determining the strengths and weaknesses of FFN care.

- There is considerable variability across FFN settings in the quality of care as there is in other types of child care. Some studies suggest that FFN child care is of lower quality than other types of child care. Other studies suggest that quality characteristics rather than type of setting are what matter in supporting positive child outcomes.

factors (e.g., educationally oriented parents may select more cognitively oriented child care centers). In addition, scientists now routinely consider the possibility that child care effects may vary by family circumstance (NICHD Early Child Care Research Network & Duncan, 2003). Another advance in child care research is the growing use of prospective, longitudinal designs that include assessments of different domains of child development (Vandell, 2004).

In spite of this progress, existing research on the quality of FFN child care is limited. FFN child care has not been defined and measured in a consistent manner across studies, and variations among FFN settings are usually not considered. We also lack representative samples of FFN care in particular and other forms of child care in general, making it impossible to generalize the findings of a specific study to the larger population in the United States. Part of the problem here is that, even though investigators have used sophisticated methods to recruit families intended to be representative of a given city or region, parents may refuse to participate and, even if they agree to participate, their child care providers may refuse to be observed. In large-scale studies completed to date, provider refusal rates range from 15% (when infants were 6 months old; NICHD Early Child Care Research Network, 1996) to 44% (Kontos et al., 1995). In the NICHD Study of Early Child Care, refusal rates were higher for informal care settings and settings caring for children of low-income families (NICHD Early Child Care Research Network, 1996), which likely led to an underestimation of child care effects associated with quality (Vandell, 2004). Refusal rates also were higher among providers in nonparental FFN and family child care settings (40%) than among providers in centers (19%) in a study of child care in poor communities (Fuller et al., 2004). A related problem is geographic differences in the supply and quality of child care (e.g., Singer, Fuller, Keiley, & Wolf, 1998). Findings from one city or region cannot be generalized to other parts of the country.

A major issue in research on FFN arrangements is the appropriateness of commonly used measures of child care quality (Maher, 2007; see also chapter 3 of this volume). One question is whether measures designed to assess quality in formal child care settings are valid and reliable tools for assessing quality in informal settings. For example, one team of researchers has expressed reservations about its use of the Family Day Care Rating Scale (Harms & Clifford, 1989) to measure the quality of FFN settings because the scale gives higher scores to settings that are formally arranged for children and in ways that resemble centers (Fuller et al., 2004). Perhaps measures used in research on parenting or family environments are more appropriate. For example, the NICHD Study of Early Child Care included an adaptation of the HOME inventory (Caldwell & Bradley, 1984), used extensively by researchers to measure the quality of home environments, as one of the observational assessments of home child care arrangements (NICHD Early Child Care Research Network, 1996). Versions of the HOME inventory have been used in other studies of family child care (Bradley, Caldwell, & Corwyn, 2003).

A related question is whether critical features of FFN settings are sufficiently represented in measures of quality frequently used in child care studies. For instance, one of the perceived characteristics of FFN child care is close, supportive ties with families. However, a systematic content analysis of seven prominent early childhood environment rating scales found that the instruments typically included few items explicitly focused on provider relationships with families (Raab & Dunst, 1997). Similarly, the child outcomes assessed in existing studies—typically cognitive, language, and social competence—may not capture some of the potential contributions of FFN care to children's development (e.g., racial and/or ethnic identity).

Lastly, most study designs do not yield information on *causal* linkages between different types or quality of child care and children's outcomes. Existing research evidence is correlational in nature because the vast majority of studies have not randomly assigned families to different child care conditions (Vandell, 2004).

With these caveats as context, studies that shed some light on the quality of FFN child care are described below. Emphasis is given to multisite investigations that included some form of FFN care as part of an examination of several types of child care. Each study recruited most or all of the sample of providers through families, thereby increasing the chances of finding often-invisible providers of FFN care. Each of the studies included structured observations (vs. parent or caregiver report only) of child care quality. Reports of the studies described here have been published in scholarly outlets that entail peer review of a study's scientific rigor.

Family Child Care and Relative Care

The most frequently cited study of the quality of FFN child care is the three-site investigation of relative care and regulated and nonregulated family child care organized by the Families and Work Institute (Galinsky et al., 1994; Kontos et al., 1995). The sample of 226 providers was recruited through a mix of methods that included use of lists of regulated providers and contact with providers identified through mothers who worked 15 hours or more per week and used a family child care provider or relative as the primary source of care for a child less than 6 years old for at least 2 consecutive months. Mothers were identified through random digit dialing and birth records. The sample was located in San Fernando/Los Angeles, Dallas/Forth Worth, and Charlotte, North Carolina. Most mothers had some college education or college degree

(62%) and were White (56%). Twenty-four percent of the mothers were African American and 17% were Hispanic. A majority (66%) of the children were less than 30 months old. In this study, there were 112 regulated family child care providers (6 were relatives of the target child or children in their care), 54 nonregulated family child care providers, and 60 relative caregivers (two thirds were the target child's grandmother, one fourth were aunts).

Overall, 13% of the regulated providers, 50% of the nonregulated providers, and 69% of the relative caregivers offered care that was classified as inadequate on the Family Day Care Rating Scale. Regulated providers were more likely to provide one or more planned activities for children per day (51%) than nonregulated providers (20%) and relative caregivers (10%). There were differences across other measures of quality, too. Overall, the regulated providers were observed to be more sensitive and to have higher levels of responsive involvement with children than relative caregivers and nonregulated family child care providers. On average, levels of observed detachment (level of interaction, interest, and supervision) were higher for relative caregivers than for nonregulated and regulated family child care providers.

Across all types of care, about one half of the children were rated as securely attached to their child care provider. Children were not more likely to be securely attached to providers who were relatives than to nonrelatives. The researchers suggested that this finding may be related to high rates of poverty (65%) among relative caregivers (e.g., their lives may be more stressful and socially isolated) and comparatively few relatives (about 25%) viewing child care as their chosen job. Across all types of care, children with more sensitive and responsive providers and in settings with good or adequate–custodial global quality were more likely to be securely attached to their providers than children in homes with inadequate global quality scores.

Although significant differences were found across the three types of care examined in this study, it is important to note the considerable range in quality within each type of care. For example, although 51% of regulated providers offered one or more planned activities for children per day, as noted above, 20% of regulated providers offered no planned activities. Further, the measures of child care quality were equally predictive of children's attachment security across all three types of care. There were no differences across the three types of providers on observed harshness in caregiver–child interactions. Also, the three types of providers did not differ in years of experience or satisfaction with their provider role (Kontos et al., 1995).

Child Care in Low-Income Communities

There are unique circumstances in the use of FFN care in the context of welfare reforms that place more stringent work requirements on parents and also enable parents to use child care subsidies for FFN care. Two recent studies provide information on the quality and influence of FFN care in low-income communities.

One study examined child care settings selected by single mothers soon after they entered welfare-to-work reform programs in 1998, when their children were between 12 and 42 months old (Loeb, Fuller, Kagan, & Carrol, 2004). The 451 families who participated in the study resided in San Francisco or San Jose, California, or Tampa, Florida. The families were evenly distributed across these three cities. The sample was racially and ethnically diverse: 41% African American, 32% Latina, and 24% White. All mothers were eligible for the federal Temporary Assistance for Needy Families (TANF) program. Interviews with mothers and child assessments were conducted in 1998 and again in 2000. Children were on average 2½ years old at the first assessment point (baseline) and an average of 4 years old at the second assessment (follow-up). FFN care was defined as nonparental kith and kin child care.

Better cognitive outcomes were found for children who participated in center-based programs than for children in FFN settings. Children's scores on tests of cognitive and language skills were significantly higher for children who were in center care at both assessment points than in FFN care at both assessments. Also, children who moved to a center program between the first and second assessments scored higher on measures of cognitive skills than children who were in FFN settings at both assessments. There were less consistent results regarding the relation of child care type to social development. Children in family child care homes tended to exhibit more behavioral problems than children in other types of care. Children in family child care homes had considerably more aggressive behaviors than children in FFN settings at both data points (Loeb et al., 2004).

The observed quality of different types of child care was analyzed in a subset of the California and Florida sample combined with a similar population of single, low-income mothers in two Connecticut cities (Fuller et al., 2004). The analysis involved 353 child care settings (166 centers, 69 family child care homes, and 118 FFN arrangements). The character and quality of FFN settings varied among sites regarding the provider's high school completion (e.g., 89% in Manchester, Connecticut, vs. 41% in San Jose, California) and the ratio of children per caregiver (e.g., 1.6 in San Francisco vs. 3.4 in Manchester and New Haven, Connecticut). Overall, the FFN providers scored low on the Family Day Care Rating Scale, which may not be an appropriate measure for FFN settings (see above). Family child care homes (which were disproportionately based in San Jose) had higher scores on the structured learning activities dimension of the Family Day Care Rating Scale than FFN arrangements. FFN providers also were less likely than family child care providers or center teachers to have completed high school. However, the quality of social interaction between caregiver and child, as measured by the Arnett (1989) Scale of Caregiver Behavior, was similar across FFN, family child care, and center settings.

The second recent study—the Welfare, Children, and Families: A Three-City Study—provides research information on one form of FFN child care in low-income communities (Votruba-Drzal, Coley, & Chase-Lansdale, 2004). Nearly one half (47%) of the study sample of 204 children was in unregulated child care homes. Other children in the study were cared for in a regulated family child care home (9%), a for-profit (9%) or nonprofit (20%) center, or Head Start program (15%). Children were between 2 and 4 years old and spent 10 or more hours per week in child care. The study examined the quality and extent of child care in relation to children's cognitive and socioemotional development over time. Families resided in low-income neighborhoods in Boston, Chicago, and San Antonio, Texas. The child sample was predominantly minority (61% African American, 30% Hispanic).

Assessments of child care quality indicated that approximately 24% of the children were in settings that provided inadequate environments for children's development, 36% were in minimally adequate arrangements, and about 40% of children were in settings rated as providing good care. In general, centers scored higher on measures of quality than regulated homes, which in turn were higher than unregulated homes. Child care characteristics were more strongly linked to children's socioemotional functioning over time than to cognitive development. Child care quality was related to reductions in children's rates of internalizing behavior and serious externalizing behavior problems. Child care quality also was related to increases in children's positive behaviors. Extensive use of child care (more than 45 hours per week) did not appear to be harmful to children except when care was of low quality. More extensive, high-quality care seemed to foster children's socioemotional functioning. Analyses suggested that the effects of child care quality did not vary by the type of care (Votruba-Drzal et al., 2004).

NICHD Study of Early Child Care

The largest prospective, longitudinal investigation of early child care conducted to date is the Study of Early Child Care, organized and funded by the National Institute of Child Health and Human Development. Data were collected at 10 research sites in major regions of the United States, including urban, suburban, and rural communities. In 1991, a sample of 1,364 families recruited through hospitals was enrolled at the time of their child's birth and to date the children have been followed through third grade. The quality of child care settings was assessed when children were 6, 15, 24, 36, and 54 months old, and observational and interview data were collected from mothers and children when children were 1, 6, 15, 24, 36, and 54 months old (NICHD Early Child Care Research Network, 2000, 2006).

With regard to FFN child care, the published results of this ambitious study do not readily map on to emerging definitions of FFN. Five types of nonmaternal care were included in the research (percentage of use at 6 months is in parentheses): father care (15%), grandparent care (17%), in-home sitter (in the child's home; 15%), child care home (provided in the caregiver's home; 35%), and child care center (18%). However, analyses involving type of care generally combine these five types of care to form three categories of child care: (a) child care center, (b) child care home (care in someone else's home by a nonrelative or a relative other than the child's grandparents), and (c) grandparent or in-home care (care in the child's home, including care by the father). Twenty-seven percent of nonrelative home care was licensed when infants were 6 months old. Most data analyses considered two types of care: the number of times a child was observed in center care, and the number of times a child was observed in child care homes. A limitation of these groupings for the purposes of this volume is that fathers are not included in most definitions of FFN child care, and both licensed and unlicensed settings are included in the child care home group.

In addition, the study excluded some families that may be prone to use FFN child care. Specifically, the study did not include families in which the mother's primary language was not English, mothers were 18 years old or younger, newborns were very ill, and families with plans to move from the area in the coming year. Of the total sample of 1,364 families at baseline, 24% of the children were minority, 11% of mothers had less than a high school education, and 14% of mothers were single (NICHD Early Child Care Research Network, 1996).

Nonetheless, study findings offer valuable understandings of child care quality and effects. Results of numerous analyses indicate that both low and high quality were found within all types of care. High quality was not an exclusive characteristic of one type of care. Further, the relation between type of care and quality varied with the age of the child. When children were 6, 15, and 24 months old, the observed quality of child care provided by relatives (fathers, grandparents, other adult relatives) in the child's or someone else's home was higher than in child care homes (next highest) or centers (lowest). At 36 months, the observed quality of relative care was only modestly higher than the quality of center care, and at 54 months there were moderate differences that favored center care over relative care and child care homes. Providers who were relatives reported higher levels of education than providers in child care homes when children were 6 months old, but the opposite was true when children were 54 months old. Center providers had the highest levels of education at all data points (NICHD Early Child Care Research Network, 2004). Higher quality child care was related to advanced cognitive, language, and preacademic outcomes at every age and better socioemotional and peer outcomes at some ages. More time in center care was related to higher cognitive and language scores and more problem and fewer prosocial behaviors, as rated by caregivers (NICHD Early Child Care Research Network, 2005, 2006).

In sum, studies offer a mixed picture of the quality of FFN child care arrangements. The most common form of nonparental care of infants and toddlers has received the least amount of research attention in comparison to formal arrangements. This state of affairs means that programs aimed at supporting FFN providers must be especially diligent in identifying and engaging a target population of informal caregivers and in securing information about and responding to their needs and interests.

Overview of Volume: Program Development and Implementation Decisions

Developers and implementers of programs designed to support caregivers in informal arrangements need to make a number of decisions in three major areas. This guide devotes a chapter to each of these areas. Here is an overview:

- Needs and interests of caregivers: Responsive programs of support begin with a solid understanding of the population they seek to serve. This information shapes decisions about program content and methods. Chapter 2 (Inside Family, Friend, and Neighbor Care) offers best guesses on unique needs and interests of FFN providers, and it suggests that programs may work best when targeted to particular subgroups of providers in informal arrangements.

- Identifying and recruiting caregivers: The invisible nature of FFN caregivers requires a series of decisions about how to find participants for a program. Chapter 3 (Finding and Engaging Family, Friend, and Neighbor Caregivers) provides guidelines for identifying and recruiting FFN caregivers for support programs, and it describes focus group and individual interview methods for gathering local information about FFN providers.

- Program content and methods: The options for addressing numerous decisions in this area—types of support to be provided, how support is offered, and who provides assistance—are described in chapter 4 (Promoting Quality in Family, Friend, and Neighbor Care).

Each program yields new learning about the opportunities and challenges of supporting FFN providers. Key lessons from programs in four diverse communities—a large suburb, an inner-city neighborhood, Somali residents of adjacent apartment complexes, and a Native American reservation—are summarized in chapter 5.

Information in this volume comes from a thin research base. Partly because the widespread interest in supporting FFN child care is new, there is limited information on strategies for finding, engaging, and supporting informal caregivers (e.g., Collins & Carlson, 1998). Most initiatives to support FFN caregivers are relatively new (developed since 2000) and only a handful of efforts have been systematically documented or assessed in relation to outcomes (Porter, 2007). More generally, research on effective approaches to training in early childhood is at an early stage of development (Maxwell, Field, & Clifford, 2006).

The guide features results of recent studies of FFN caregivers gathered through statewide surveys and focus groups. It also highlights the efforts of several ambitious initiatives aimed at supporting informal caregivers. These include Early Head Start's Enhanced Home Visiting Pilot Project (Paulsell, Mekos, Del Grosso, Banghart, & Nogales, 2006); Sparking Connections, a collaborative demonstration and evaluation project of the Families and Work Institute (O'Donnell et al., 2006); and the Archibald Bush Foundation's projects to support FFN infant–toddler caregivers in diverse communities (see chapter 5).

References

Anderson, S. G., Ramsburg, D. M., & Scott, J. (2005). *Illinois study of license-exempt child care: Final report.* Springfield, IL: Illinois Department of Human Services.

Arnett, J. (1989). Caregivers in day-care centers: Does training matter? *Journal of Applied Developmental Psychology, 10,* 541–552.

Bradley, R. H., Caldwell, B. M., & Corwyn, R. F. (2003). The child care HOME Inventories: Assessing the quality of family child care homes. *Early Childhood Research Quarterly, 18,* 294–309.

Brandon, R. N., Maher, E. J., Joesch, J. M., & Doyle, S. (2002). *Understanding family, friend, and neighbor care in Washington state: Developing appropriate training and support.* Seattle: Human Services Policy Center, Evans School of Public Affairs, University of Washington.

Brandon, R. N., & Martinez-Beck, I. (2006). Estimating the size and characteristics of the United States early care and education workforce. In M. Zaslow & I. Martinez-Beck (Eds.), *Critical issues in early childhood professional development* (pp. 49–76). Baltimore: Brookes.

Caldwell, B. M., & Bradley, R. H. (1984). *Home observation for measurement of the environment.* Little Rock: University of Arkansas at Little Rock.

Capizzano, J., & Adams, G. (2003). *Snapshots of America's families: Children in low-income families are less likely to be in center-based child care.* Rep. No. 16. Washington, DC: Urban Institute.

Chase, R., Arnold, J., Schauben, L., & Shardlow, B. (2005). *Child care use in Minnesota: 2004 statewide household child care survey.* St. Paul, MN: Wilder Research. Retrieved November 3, 2006, from http://edocs.dhs.state.mn.us/lfserver/Legacy/DHS-4623-ENG

Clampet-Lundquist, S., Edin, K., London, A., Scott, E., & Hunter, V. (2004). "Making a way out of no way": How mothers meet basic family needs while moving from welfare to work. In A. C. Crouter & A. Booth (Ed.), *Work-family challenges for low-income parents and their children* (pp. 203–241). Mahwah, NJ: Erlbaum.

Collins, A., & Carlson, B. (1998). Child care by kith and kin—supporting family, friends, and neighbors caring for children. *Children and Welfare Reform, Issue Brief 5.* New York: National Center for Children in Poverty, Mailman School of Public Health, Columbia University.

Early, D. M., & Burchinal, M. R. (2001). Early childhood care: Relations with family characteristics and preferred care characteristics. *Early Childhood Research Quarterly, 16,* 475–497.

Emerita, B. (2006). *Family, friend, and neighbor care best practices in diverse communities: How families are teaching their children to succeed.* Minneapolis, MN: Ready 4 K.

Fuller, B., Kagan, S. L., Loeb, S., & Chang, Y. (2004). Child care quality: Centers and home settings that serve poor families. *Early Childhood Research Quarterly, 19*, 505–527.

Galinsky, E., Howes, C., Kontos, S., & Shinn, M. (1994). *The study of children in family child care and relative care: Highlights of findings.* New York: Families and Work Institute.

Gordon, J. (2000). How our field participates in undermining quality in child care. *Young Children, 55*, 31–34.

Greenberg, M. H., Levin-Epstein, J., Hutson, R. Q., Ooms, T. J., Schumacher, R., Turetsky, V., et al. (2001). The 1996 welfare law: Key elements and reauthorization issues affecting children. *Future of Children, 12*, 27–57.

Han, W.-J. (2004). Nonstandard work schedules and child care decisions: Evidence from the NICHD Study of Early Child Care. *Early Childhood Research Quarterly, 19*, 231–256.

Harms, T., & Clifford, R. M. (1989). *Family day care rating scale.* New York: Teachers College Press.

Johnson, J. O. (2005, October). *Who's minding the kids? Child care arrangements: Winter 2002.* Washington, DC: U.S. Census Bureau.

Kreader, J. L., Ferguson, D., & Lawrence, S. (2005, April). Infant and toddler child care arrangements. *Research-to-Policy Connections, No. 1.* New York: National Center for Children in Poverty, Columbia University. (Available at www.childcareresearch.org)

Kreader, J. L., & Lawrence, S. (2006, September). *Toward a national strategy to improve family, friend, and neighbor child care. Report of a symposium.* New York: National Center for Children in Poverty, Columbia University.

Kontos, S., Howes, C., Shinn, M., & Galinsky, E. (1995). *Quality in family child care and relative care.* New York: Teachers College Press.

Loeb, S., Fuller, B., Kagan, S. L., & Carrol, B. (2004). Child care in poor communities: Early learning effects of type, quality, and stability. *Child Development, 75*, 47–65.

Maxwell, K. L., Field, C. C., & Clifford, R. M. (2006). Defining and measuring professional development in early childhood research. In M. Zaslow & I. Martinez-Beck (Eds.), *Critical issues in early childhood professional development* (pp. 21–48). Baltimore: Brookes.

Maher, E. J. (2007, April). Measuring quality in family, friend, and neighbor child care: Conceptual and practical issues. *Research-to-Policy Connections, No. 6.* New York: National Center for Children in Poverty, Columbia University. (Available at www.researchconnections.org)

Mulligan, G. M., Brimhall, D., West, J., & Chapman, C. (2005). *Child care and early education arrangements of infants, toddlers, and preschoolers: 2001.* Washington, DC: National Household Education Surveys Program, National Center for Education Statistics, U.S. Department of Education.

Myers, S. (n.d.). *Minnesota Sparking Connections: Child care resource and referral strategies for supporting family, friend, and neighbor caregivers.* St. Paul, MN: Minnesota Child Care Resource and Referral Network.

NICHD Early Child Care Research Network. (1996). Characteristics of infant child care: Factors contributing to positive caregiving. *Early Childhood Research Quarterly, 11,* 269–306.

NICHD Early Child Care Research Network. (1997). Familial factors associated with the characteristics of nonmaternal care for infants. *Journal of Marriage and the Family, 59,* 389–408.

NICHD Early Child Care Research Network. (2000). Characteristics and quality of child care for toddlers and preschoolers. *Applied Developmental Sciences, 4,* 116–135.

NICHD Early Child Care Research Network. (2004). Type of child care and children's development at 54 months. *Early Childhood Research Quarterly, 19,* 203–230.

NICHD Early Child Care Research Network. (2005). Early child care and children's development in the primary grades: Follow-up results from the NICHD Study of Early Child Care. *American Educational Research Journal, 42,* 537–570.

NICHD Early Child Care Research Network. (2006). Child care effect sizes for the NICHD Study of Early Child Care and Youth Development. *American Psychologist, 61,* 99–116.

NICHD Early Child Care Research Network, & Duncan, G. J. (2003). Modeling the impacts of child care quality on children's preschool cognitive development. *Child Development, 74,* 1454–1475.

O'Donnell, N. S., Cochran, M., Lekies, K., Diehl, D., Morrissey, T. W., Ashley, N., et al. (2006). *Sparking Connections, Phase II: A multi-site evaluation of community-based strategies to support family, friend and neighbor caregivers of children. Part 1: Lessons learned and recommendations.* New York: Families and Work Institute.

Paulsell, D., Mekos, D., Del Grosso, P., Banghart, P., & Nogales, R. (2006). *The Enhanced Home Visiting Pilot Project: How Early Head Start programs are reaching out to kith and kin caregivers.* Final interim report submitted to the U.S. Department of Health and Human Services, Administration of Children, Youth and Families, Head Start Bureau. Princeton, NJ: Mathematica Policy Research.

Porter, T. (2007, March). Assessing initiatives for family, friend, and neighbor child care. *Research-to-Policy Connections, No. 5.* New York: National Center for Children in Poverty, Columbia University. (Available at www.researchconnections.org)

Pungello, E., & Kurtz-Costes, B. (1999). Why and how working women choose child care: A review with a focus on infancy. *Developmental Review, 19,* 31–96.

Raab, M. M., & Dunst, C. J. (1997). Early childhood program assessment scales and family support practices. In S. Reifel (Series Ed.), C. J. Dunst & M. Wolery (Vol. Eds.), *Advances in early education and day care. Vol. 9: Family policy and practice in early child care* (pp. 105–131). Greenwich, CT: JAI Press.

Singer, J. D., Fuller, B., Keiley, M. K., & Wolf, A. (1998). Early child-care selection: Variation by geographic location, maternal characteristics, and family structure. *Developmental Psychology, 34,* 1129–1144.

Snyder, K., & Adelman, S. (2004). *The use of relative care while parents work: Findings from the 1999 National Survey of America's Families.* Washington, DC: Urban Institute.

Snyder, K., Dore, T., & Adelman, S. (2005). *Use of relative care by working parents. Snapshots of America's families, No. 23.* Washington, DC: Urban Institute.

Susman-Stillman, A. (2005, November). *Current research directions in family, friend, and neighbor care: An interim report.* Paper presented at Improving Family, Friend, and Neighbor Care: Toward a National Strategy symposium, hosted by National Center for Children in Poverty. Baltimore.

Vandell, D. L. (2004). Early child care: The known and the unknown. *Merrill-Palmer Quarterly, 50,* 387–414.

Votruba-Drzal, E., Coley, E. L., & Chase-Lansdale, P. L. (2004). Child care and low-income children's development: Direct and moderated effects. *Child Development, 75,* 296–312.

Zaslow, M., & Martinez-Beck, I. (Eds.). (2006). *Critical issues in early childhood professional development.* Baltimore: Brookes.

Zinsser, C. (1991). *Raised in East Urban: Child care in a working class community.* New York: Teachers College Press.

Zinsser, C. (2001). Child care within the family. *Future of Children, 11,* 123–127.

Chapter 2

Inside Family, Friend, and Neighbor Care

*A*n ambitious effort to provide high-quality early care and education services to children ages birth to 5 years in 80 low-income neighborhoods in Pittsburgh and surrounding parts of Allegheny County, Pennsylvania, was launched in 1996. The program, known as the Early Childhood Initiative, sought to be the first in the nation to establish a comprehensive system for delivering high-quality child care on a countywide basis. Carried out under the auspices of the United Way of Allegheny County, the initiative called for each of the targeted neighborhoods to have control over its particular early childhood programs through local neighborhood agencies that would choose and supervise early education and care services at the community level (Gill, Dembosky, & Caulkins, 2002).

Several community planning groups within the initiative attempted to recruit unregulated family child care homes to participate in the program. Getting providers to attend meetings or express an interest in the initiative proved to be difficult, however. Some unregulated providers initially considered joining the program but lost interest once they learned that participation included the completion of a 50-hour preservice training course, 24 hours of additional training each year, home inspections, and observations by quality assurance monitors. Some providers started but did not complete the preservice training component, whereas some others completed the 50-hour preservice course but dropped out during the home inspection phase, which involved the development of improvement plans (Gill et al., 2002).

The Allegheny County program's inability to enroll large numbers of family child care providers limited the reach of the initiative to mostly center-based care, thereby missing the significant portion of children who were in the care of relatives, friends, or neighbors. Evaluators observed that the initiative's experience was not unusual: "We know of no program that has solved the problem of getting substantial numbers of unregulated...providers to join a high-quality, regulated system" (Gill et al., 2002, p. 79).

The lesson of the child care improvement initiative in Allegheny County and numerous other communities is that there is minimal benefit in attempting to improve the quality of family, friend, and neighbor (FFN) child care by trying to incorporate informal caregivers into formal systems of child care training and regulation. This strategy may appeal to a small segment of the FFN population. For most FFN providers, meaningful support of their caregiver role is more likely to emerge from a program development process that begins with a careful recognition of the realities of informal care arrangements.

This chapter offers best guesses about characteristics of FFN child care that deserve attention in designing programs of support for informal caregivers. As indicated in chapter 1, research on FFN child care is limited. Programs aimed at supporting FFN child care will want to gather their own information to guide local program planning (see chapter 3 for strategies). This chapter provides a "what to look for" overview of qualities of FFN child care. Attention is given to unique tasks of FFN caregiving and to differences among FFN caregivers.

Unique Dimensions of FFN Caregiving

FFN caregivers face distinctive tasks in at least three areas: parent–caregiver relationships, child–caregiver relationships, and health and safety.

Parent–Caregiver Relationships

Mutually supportive relationships between parents and other caregivers are a core feature of high-quality child care arrangements (Powell, 2001). Experts agree that infants and toddlers benefit when parents and caregivers work to establish continuity and connections between parent and caregiver by, for example, communicating daily about the child's activities, needs, and accomplishments (e.g., Lally et al., 2003).

Relationships between caregivers and parents are qualitatively different in FFN child care compared to other types of care. A defining characteristic of FFN care is that the arrangement is embedded in the caregiver's extended family and friendship network. The caregiver has a history of relations with the child and the child's family, and interpersonal connections usually continue long after the caregiver stops providing regular child care. The child care arrangement, then, is one point in a long history of relationships.

Reciprocity in giving and receiving help seems to be a factor for many caregivers. In a focus group study, for example, a grandfather indicated that "If I help them take care of their children, they will certainly treat me better," and a person caring for a neighbor's infant explained that the child's mother had "supported me good" at an earlier point when she was going through a difficult time (Porter, Rice, & Mabon, 2003, p. 24).

For many parents and FFN caregivers, the child care arrangement appears to add value to their existing ties. A sizeable percentage of parents (39%) and FFN caregivers (48%) in a large Illinois study indicated that their relationships with one another had improved as a result of caregiving interactions, and nearly all others reported no change in the quality of their relationships (Anderson, Ramsburg, & Scott, 2005). Focus group research has found a similar pattern (Porter et al., 2003).

The cultural continuity and interpersonal connectedness of most informal care arrangements provide a foundation for close collaborations between caregivers and parents. The fact that FFN caregivers and parents usually represent similar background characteristics does not mean their relationships exist without stress, however. Caregiver–parent interactions are complex in any setting (e.g., Powell, 1997). The warmth and informality of home-based settings may add complexity to relationships, making it easier than in centers, for example, for parents to arrive late to pick up their child if they see the caregiver as someone who is home anyway (Kontos, 1992). Results of recent research on FFN arrangements suggest that some caregivers may welcome assistance in setting boundaries, communicating, and resolving conflicts with parents.

Boundaries. Relationships between child care providers and parents in home-based arrangements have long been identified as more supportive than relationships in center care (e.g., Hughes, 1985; Pence & Goelman, 1987). In FFN arrangements, roles often have blurred boundaries. The caregivers are more than child care providers. They relate to the parent in a role as mother, sister, aunt, father, or long-time friend or neighbor and in a role as significant partner in child-rearing responsibilities and perhaps other idiosyncratic roles (e.g., loaner of money). Similarly, the parent has counterpart roles (i.e., daughter, sister, friend). Many caregivers advise parents about child-rearing matters, particularly when caregivers are grandmothers caring for their daughter's children. The giving of advice—regardless of whether it has been requested—seems to be viewed as a prerogative of the caregiver's relationship to the parent (Porter et al., 2003). For example, one grandmother told researchers, "That's one thing I'm trying to teach my daughter. When she had the baby at three weeks I was trying to tell her that you have to have a routine with the baby" (Porter et al., 2003, p. 22). It seems that support often flows in both directions. Most FFN caregivers in one study reported that they primarily get encouragement and emotional support from family members (91%) and parents (90%) of the children in their care (Chase, Arnold, Schauben, & Shardlow, 2006).

Some may like this fluidity, others may not. For instance, one FFN provider caring for her niece found it helpful to separate the FFN arrangement from their family relationships by viewing her sister (the child's mother) as her "business partner" during the times care was being provided and as her sister ("we're best friends") during family times. She insisted that baby-sitting issues be discussed before or after child care, not at family gatherings (Porter et al., 2003, p. 24). This separation of business and pleasure can be challenging to negotiate in the absence of an organizational framework (e.g., center policies) and in the context of existing family or friend relationships.

Communication. In general, FFN caregivers and parents apparently maintain positive relationships. For example, a large majority of FFN caregivers (85%) in a recent Minnesota survey indicated that they and parents cooperate and work together "very well" to meet the needs of children in the providers' care. A closer look suggests there is some room for improvement, however, especially among nonrelative care-givers. A majority of FFN caregivers (61%) indicated that they talk frequently with parents about the child's daily activities; relative care-givers of children age 5 years and younger were more likely than other caregivers to discuss daily activities. Relatives were more likely than nonrelatives to have strong partnerships with the child's parents (64% vs. 43%; Chase, Arnold, Schauben, & Shardlow, 2006).

The converse of the communication patterns described here suggests that nearly 40% of caregivers do not talk frequently with parents about the child's daily activities, and that 57% of nonrelative caregivers and 36% of relative caregivers do not have strong partnerships with parents (e.g., frequently share information about the child, cooperate very well).

Resolving conflicts. Results of most but not all studies of FFN care suggest that conflicts between caregivers and parents are not common (e.g., Anderson et al., 2005). In the Minnesota survey, 87% of FFN caregivers indicated that the match between their child-rearing values and those of the parents was excellent or good (Chase, Arnold, Schauben, & Shardlow, 2006). However, when conflicts occur, the issue often pertains to discipline, with caregivers reporting that they tend to be stricter than parents with the child (e.g., "She will let him do anything...." Porter et al., 2003, p. 23). Some caregivers told researchers that they try to work out discipline disagreements with parents through mutual discussion (Anderson et al., 2005), whereas other caregivers indicated that they simply did not pursue the matter and often continue with the child care arrangement despite unresolved conflicts (Porter et al., 2003).

Differences between parents and FFN caregivers regarding child behavior expectations were among the top concerns and challenges identified by FFN providers in half or more of 37 focus groups convened in a recent California study. For example, some caregivers noted that children have less structure and different rules with their parents, leading to misbehavior at home that often carries over into the child care setting (Drake, Unti, Greenspoon, & Fawcett, 2004).

FFN arrangements involving grandmothers may pose unique challenges for recognizing and addressing conflicts. A study of rural employed mothers whose young children were regularly in the care of their grandmothers found that the psychological benefits of grandmother care (e.g., complete trust) were just as significant in the eyes of mothers as the practical advantages (e.g., flexible hours, provision of care for ill child). Some mothers viewed their own mother as a coparent ("my other half when it comes to parenting") and thought the care arrangement was a positive influence on intergenerational relationships (Reschke & Walker, 2005, p. 35). At the same time, the closeness of these bonds may entail grandmother interference in her daughter's parenting role or may constrain mothers from recognizing or raising concerns about the arrangement. Mothers may fear that criticism might be perceived as ungrateful behavior or might put the arrangement and other types of support at risk (Reschke & Walker, 2005).

Studies consistently show that most FFN caregivers—particularly relatives—do not receive money from parents for providing care (Brandon, Maher, Joesch, & Doyle, 2002; Chase, Arnold, Schauben, & Shardlow, 2006). There is limited information on how the presence or absence of money contributes to relationship quality. Do parents feel less able to voice concerns when they do not pay or do not adequately pay an informal caregiver? Under what conditions do caregivers feel exploited? Or do altruistic purposes and norms of reciprocity generally prevail? And when money does change hands, are arrangements handled in a mutually satisfactory manner?

What's Different About Family, Friend, and Neighbor Care?

- Family, friend, and neighbor (FFN) care arrangements are embedded in the caregiver's extended family and friendship network.

    —The caregiver has a history and a future of relationships with the child and the child's family.

    —Reciprocity in giving and receiving help seems especially important. Most relative caregivers and many neighbor and friend caregivers do not receive money for providing care.

    —The above factors may pose unique challenges for caregivers and parents in setting boundaries, communicating, and resolving conflicts.

- FFN settings often entail exceptionally close interpersonal relationships.

    —FFN caregivers generally communicate deep attachment to the children in their care.

    —Other children in the setting are likely to be members of the same family or the caregiver's family or both.

    —The age span of children in an FFN arrangement may be greater than typically found in family child care homes and centers.

- Whether some health and safety requirements for licensed facilities are appropriate to FFN settings is debatable.

    —For example, expert recommendations for infant feeding may not coincide with culturally driven practices in some FFN settings.

Child–Caregiver Relationships

Warm, responsive relationships between caregivers and young children are consistently viewed by experts as an essential feature of child care quality (Lally et al., 2003; Lamb & Ahnert, 2006). Parents, too, consider closeness in the child–caregiver relationship as a key attribute of FFN arrangements, particularly when relatives care for their children (Zinsser, 2001).

Caregivers also value close relationships with children in their care. In focus groups, many caregivers have emphasized their love for the children in their care and the special relationship they share. This portrayal of caregiver–child relationships is especially common among grandmothers and aunts (Porter et al., 2003). Most FFN caregivers communicate deep attachment to the children in their care, and they describe how the children enjoy being with them. For example, a grandmother caring for her 2½-year-old grandson told researchers, "He just loves me, just loves being in my house. He sees me, his eyes light up and he runs and just jumps in my arms" (Porter et al., 2003, p. 15). Friend and neighbor caregivers also express strong attachments to children and their parents.

The reports of love and affection in focus group research indirectly support the idea that child–caregiver attachments are stronger in relative FFN settings than in home-based care by nonrelatives. The three-site study of family child care and relative care led by the Families and Work Institute, described in chapter 1, did not find this to be the case. Children were no more likely to be attached to relatives than to nonrelative caring for children in licensed and unlicensed homes (Kontos, Howes, Shinn, & Galinsky, 1995).

In recent surveys, many FFN providers have indicated interest in receiving information on child development, activities for children (Anderson et al., 2005), and ways to help children learn (Chase, Arnold, Schauben, & Shardlow, 2006). Results of studies on the quality of FFN care offer useful clues on specific types of information that might be helpful to caregivers. These findings are summarized below.

Interactions and activities. Caregivers' positive interactions with children were strengths of the FFN settings observed in a Minnesota exploratory study. Caregivers displayed interest in children, affection, responsiveness, and helpfulness. They talked with children, responded to their speech, and did not use harsh words or actions. They encouraged children's appropriate actions and acknowledged their efforts. The FFN caregivers in this study also provided age-appropriate activities, including ample opportunities to play and explore their environments. There were materials to promote language and dramatic play, and some books were accessible (Tout & Zaslow, 2006).

FFN caregivers participating in focus group research report that they frequently sing with children, coo to infants, engage in conversations with toddlers, and elaborate on young children's language attempts. Reading with children appears to be a regular activity. Hugging and kissing are reportedly common (Porter et al., 2003).

Observational research suggests there are opportunities for growth in the quality of children's daily experiences in FFN care. In the Minnesota study, caregivers missed opportunities to talk with children about their emotions and help children express their feelings, particularly when upset. They also did not consistently promote cooperative play, sharing, or taking turns when two or more children were present. There also were missed opportunities to support and extend children's learning by talking with children about their play and introducing new activities. About one third of the settings provided children with opportunities to engage in making music or creative movement. Books were in most of the homes, but only about one third of the settings had 10 or more age-appropriate books. Further, caregivers did not limit television use and did not turn off the television when children were not watching it. The content of television viewing was appropriate in nearly all of the settings, however (Tout & Zaslow, 2006).

The researchers recommend that assistance to caregivers emphasize strategies for developing simple plans for their care of children, not in the form of a detailed daily schedule or lesson plan, but activities and interactions that would provide the types of experiences they want children to have in their setting. The researchers also suggest that caregivers be given information on the importance of limiting television use, and on how children's emotional competence and social skills are important dimensions of school readiness (Tout & Zaslow, 2006).

Familial ties in multiage settings. Two dimensions of many FFN child care arrangements need to be recognized in quality improvement strategies: (a) the likelihood that other children in the setting are members of the same family or the caregiver's family or both, and (b) the range of child ages.

A sizeable minority of FFN caregivers have one or more of their own children under age 13 with them while providing child care. For example, 24% of respondents in a recent Illinois survey were in this situation, and 25% of the providers indicated that being able to stay home with their own children was among their motivations for providing FFN care (Anderson et al., 2005). Some FFN providers also care for several children who are members of the same family (i.e., the children are siblings) or the same extended family (i.e., the children are cousins).

Information about this dynamic situation is scant, but it seems reasonable to assume that some caregivers would benefit from assistance on how to manage the various relational systems. For instance, a caregiver may need guidance on how to help her own child share his mother with another child (who is not a sibling but may be a cousin) on a regular basis. Caregivers also may need help in how to divide and prioritize their attention across different children.

Multiage settings are common in formal early childhood programs, but typically the ages span no more than several years (e.g., a classroom of 3- to 5-year-olds). An FFN arrangement may include an infant or toddler plus a preschool-age child and/or a school-age child during nonschool times. One implication for an FFN support program is that caregivers may be interested in ideas about how to handle the opportunities and challenges of a mixed-age setting in terms of planning activities and distributing caregiver time across children. Another implication of the multiage setting is that caregivers may want information on a range of child ages. A program focused on the care of infants and toddlers exclusively or primarily may be viewed as limited (see chapters 4 and 5).

Health and Safety

Good safety and health provisions, including nutritional meals, are a common focus of quality improvement efforts targeted to both formal and informal child care. For years the American Academy of Pediatrics and other organizations have set standards and provided resources on health and safety (e.g., Murph, Palmer, & Glassy, 2005), and this domain is a primary focus of child care licensing standards and supports.

Parents want safe environments for their young children, of course, and surveys of FFN providers consistently show that caregivers want training in CPR and other health and safety areas (Anderson et al., 2005; Chase, Arnold, Schauben, & Shardlow, 2006). There appears to be no debate in the FFN literature on the applicability of some basic elements of child care health and safety standards to informal settings (e.g., keep poisons out of child reach). Questions have been raised about the relevance of some other standards, however. Expert recommendations for infant feeding may not be supportive of cultural traditions embraced in some FFN settings, for instance. Also, should FFN caregivers conduct regular fire drills as required in most regulated family child care homes and centers? (Porter & Rice, 2000).

The Minnesota study of FFN child care found that many safety precautions were in place. A majority of homes had smoke detectors, for example; equipment was in good repair, and meals included opportunities to learn self-help skills and to engage in conversations. However, electrical outlets were not consistently covered, stairs were not always secured, and hazardous items were accessible to children in lower cupboards or on open shelves. Consistent hand washing—by caregiver and children before and after preparing food and eating, and after using the bathroom or changing diapers—also was in need of attention (Tout & Zaslow, 2006).

Differences Among FFN Caregivers

FFN caregivers are a diverse group. In addition to differences in the caregiver's relationship to the child (relative, friend, or neighbor), there are variations in the frequency, duration, and scope of care arrangements. Grandparents who care for their infant–toddler grandchildren, for example,

Types of Assistance Caregivers May Welcome

Family, friend, and neighbor (FFN) caregivers may welcome help in the following areas:

- Maintaining positive parent–caregiver relationships
  - Dealing creatively with the multiple roles of participants in FFN settings (e.g., grandmother, mother, daughter, giver of advice, loaner of money)
  - Communicating frequently about the child's daily activities
  - Resolving conflicts, particularly differences in dealing with children's behaviors
- Fostering warm, responsive relationships with children
  - Talking with children about their play and introducing new activities
  - Limiting television viewing
  - Promoting children's social–emotional development
  - Facilitating children's experiences in a mixed-age care setting with children who share close ties to the caregiver
- Maintaining good health and safety provisions
  - Ensuring a safe environment (e.g., covering electrical outlets, securing stairways, and consistently washing hands)

differ in whether care is provided on a regular full-time, a regular part-time, or a sporadic basis (Vandell, McCartney, Owen, Booth, & Clarke-Stewart, 2003).

One form of outreach and support is unlikely to appeal or be useful to all caregivers. A major challenge is to identify meaningful differences among FFN caregivers that can help define essential features of responsive approaches to engaging and supporting FFN providers. The task of determining what types of support would be beneficial to which subgroups of informal providers is uncharted territory. There are many ways to unpack the FFN population. Several approaches are described below as examples.

Tailoring to Subgroups of Family, Friend, and Neighbor Caregivers

Outreach to family, friend, and neighbor (FFN) caregivers may be more effective when it is tailored to particular subgroups of informal providers:

- Relative caregivers in general may value a program of support that embraces their reason for becoming an informal provider: to help out a family member.

 —Most relative caregivers probably see little value in "child care training" because few family caregivers view themselves as child care providers or wish to become licensed providers.

- Offering a customary child care training program to informal child care providers may appeal to the following:

 —Friend and neighbor caregivers because often they are similar to regulated child care providers in their reason for becoming an informal provider—to stay home with their own children or grandchildren.

 —Caregivers who receive a government subsidy for providing child care because they are already connected to a formal child care system and many are interested in becoming licensed providers.

 —Extending FFN support programs primarily or exclusively to those who receive a government subsidy is likely to reach a small segment of the larger population of FFN caregivers. A vast majority of FFN caregivers do not receive a government subsidy for providing child care.

Family Versus Friend and Neighbor Caregivers

One promising idea is to recognize that the orientation of relatives to their caregiver role may differ from the orientation of friends and neighbors (Chase, 2006). This suggestion is based on research indicating that, among informal providers, relatives tend to approach their child care work differently than friends and neighbors.

A consistent finding of studies conducted in different parts of the United States is that approximately 60% to 75% of FFN caregivers indicate they became a provider to help out a family member or friend. In contrast, between 20% and 25% of FFN providers cite a child-oriented reason (e.g., "I like children and it's fun"; Brandon et al., 2002; Chase, Arnold, Schauben, & Shardlow, 2006; Galinsky et al., 1994).

More relatives than friend and neighbor caregivers cite adult-focused motivations. In several studies, relative caregivers were more likely than nonrelative caregivers to indicate that their main reason for becoming a provider was to help a family member or friend (e.g., 61% vs. 53% in the Minnesota study; Chase, Arnold, Schauben, & Shardlow, 2006), and nonrelative caregivers were more likely than relative caregivers to cite child-oriented reasons (Galinsky et al., 1994). In one study, a majority of nonregulated friend and neighbor caregivers were more like regulated providers in their primary reason for becoming providers—to stay home with own children and/or grandchildren—and were less like a majority of relative caregivers, whose primary reason was to help the child's mother (Galinsky et al., 1994). Especially important here is research evidence indicating that the quality of care is generally lower when individuals (both licensed and legally unlicensed) become providers to help out mothers.

Subsidized Versus Unsubsidized Informal Caregivers

Whether an informal caregiver receives a government subsidy for providing child care is another promising way to identify meaningful differences among FFN caregivers. FFN caregivers who receive a government subsidy seem to show more signs of movement toward a professional role than caregivers who do not receive a subsidy. They may be interested in a longer term role as a caregiver of other people's children, and they may be interested in becoming a licensed child care provider. What began as an extension of parenting may have triggered interest in the broader field and work of child care.

For example, 52% of FFN providers caring for children through the Minnesota child care assistance program expressed interest in getting licensed as a child care provider compared with 18% of FFN caregivers overall. Also, 66% of caregivers receiving a subsidy indicated it would be "very helpful" to have access to a government subsidized food program compared with 30% of FFN caregivers overall (Chase, Arnold, & Schauben, 2006; Chase, Arnold, Schauben, & Shardlow, 2006). Of the subsidized unlicensed providers in Illinois, 58% were very interested or somewhat interested in becoming licensed providers, though most indicated they knew little about licensing (Anderson et al., 2005). In the survey of the general population of FFN providers in the state of Washington, only 15% of caregivers expressed interest in becoming a licensed child care provider (Brandon et al., 2002).

Among friend and neighbor caregivers, reasons for becoming a provider differed somewhat between subsidized providers and the general population of FFN caregivers in Minnesota studies. Nearly 30% of nonrelative providers caring for children in the child care assistance program (Chase, Arnold, & Schauben, 2006) compared to 53% of nonrelative providers in the general population of FFN caregivers (Chase, Arnold, Schauben, & Shardlow, 2006) indicated that they were providing child care to help a family member or friend. Nearly 50% of subsidized non-relative providers (Chase, Arnold, & Schauben, 2006) versus nearly 30% of nonrelative caregivers in the general FFN population (Chase, Arnold, Schauben, & Shardlow, 2006) cited a child-focused reason. More relatives in the general FFN population (20%) than subsidized relatives (11%) cited a child-focused reason, but the percentage of rela-tive providers citing adult-focused reasons were similar in both samples (61% general, 64% subsidized; Chase, Arnold, & Schauben, 2006; Chase, Arnold, Schauben, & Shardlow, 2006). Because participants in the Minnesota study of subsidized FFN caregivers were drawn from selected counties, caution must be used in comparing results to the statewide sample of the general FFN population.

One practical significance of the subsidized versus unsubsidized distinction is that FFN providers who receive a government subsidy are typically the primary or sole focus of state initiatives aimed at improving the quality of informal child care (Porter & Kearns, 2005). This subgroup of FFN caregivers is easy to locate and, in general, is probably likely to see value in child care training and resources linked to licensure. The problem is that this subgroup is a small minority of FFN caregivers. For example, only 4.8% of all FFN providers in the Minnesota survey indicated that they received money from a county or state agency (Chase, Arnold, Schauben, & Shardlow, 2006), and 9% of children with FFN care as the primary arrangement in the state of Washington survey were receiving financial assistance (Brandon et al., 2002).

In sum, this chapter has sought to "unpack" the broad category of FFN child care by identifying unique tasks of FFN caregivers and differences among informal providers. As suggested in the chapter's introduction, attempts to reach FFN caregivers by simply extending existing systems of support for licensed child care programs are likely to be successful for a small segment of FFN providers at best. The easiest-to-locate providers (i.e., those receiving a child care subsidy) do not represent the full range of FFN caregivers. What is more, diversity within the world of FFN child care suggests that "one size fits all" approaches to promoting quality in FFN care may not be optimally responsive. The interests and needs of grandmothers and other relatives may be quite different from the circumstances of other informal providers. This chapter provides some frameworks for program developers to consider in figuring out how to implement a long-standing principle in the human services: begin where the client is (Provence, Naylor, & Patterson, 1977).

References

Anderson, S. G., Ramsburg, D. M., & Scott, J. (2005). *Illinois study of license-exempt child care: Final report.* Springfield, IL: Illinois Department of Human Services.

Brandon, R. N., Maher, E. J., Joesch, J. M., & Doyle, S. (2002). *Understanding family, friend, and neighbor care in Washington state: Developing appropriate training and support.* Seattle: Human Services Policy Center, Evans School of Public Affairs, University of Washington.

Chase, R. (2006, March). *Quality, quality improvement & school readiness.* Panel presentation at the Minnesota Child Care Research Partnership Forum on "Using the evidence: Policy implications of recent child care and early education research." Minneapolis, MN.

Chase, R., Arnold, J., & Schauben, L. (2006). *Family, friends and neighbors caring for children through the Minnesota Child Care Assistance Program.* St. Paul, MN: Wilder Research. Retrieved November 3, 2006, from http://edocs.dhs.state.mn.us/lfserver/ Legacy/DHS-4517-ENG

Chase, R., Arnold, J., Schauben, L., & Shardlow, B. (2006). *Family, friend and neighbor caregivers: Results of the 2004 Minnesota statewide household child care survey.* St. Paul, MN: Wilder Research. Retrieved November 3, 2006, from http://edocs.dhs.state.mn.us/lfserver/Legacy/DHS-4516-ENG

Drake, P. J., Unti, L., Greenspoon, B., & Fawcett, L. K. (2004). *First Five California informal child caregiver support project: Focus groups and interviews report.* Sacramento, CA: First 5 California Children and Families Commission and ETS Associates.

Galinsky, E., Howes, C., Kontos, S., & Shinn, M. (1994). *The study of children in family child care and relative care: Highlights of findings.* New York: Families and Work Institute.

Gill, B. P., Dembosky, J. W., & Caulkins, J. P. (2002). *A "noble bet" in early care and education: Lessons from one community's experience.* Santa Monica, CA: RAND.

Hughes, R. (1985). The informal help-giving of home and center childcare providers. *Family Relations, 34,* 359–366.

Kontos, S. (1992). *Family day care: Out of the shadows and into the limelight.* Washington, DC: National Association for the Education of Young Children.

Kontos, S., Howes, C., Shinn, M., & Galinsky, E. (1995). *Quality in family child care and relative care.* New York: Teachers College Press.

Lally, R., Griffin, A., Fenichel, E., Segal, M., Szanton, E., & Weissbourd, B. (2003). *Caring for infants and toddlers in groups: Developmentally appropriate practice.* Washington, DC: ZERO TO THREE.

Lamb, M. E., & Ahnert, L. (2006). Nonparental child care: Context, concepts, correlates, and consequences. In W. Damon & R. W. Lerner (Series Eds.) & K. A. Renninger & I. E. Sigel (Vol. Eds.), *Handbook of child psychology: Vol. 4. Child psychology in practice* (6th ed., pp. 950–1016). New York: Wiley.

Murph, J. R., Palmer, S. S., & Glassy, D. (Eds.). (2005). *Health in child care: A manual for health professionals* (4th ed.). Elk Grove Village, IL: American Academy of Pediatrics.

Pence, A. R., & Goelman, H. (1987). Silent partners: Parents of children in three types of day care. *Early Childhood Research Quarterly, 2,* 103–118.

Porter, T., & Kearns, S. M. (2005). *Supporting family, friend and neighbor caregivers: Findings from a survey of state policies.* New York: Institute for a Child Care Continuum, Bank Street College of Education.

Porter, T., & Rice, R. (2000). *Lessons learned: Strategies for working with kith and kin caregivers.* New York: Institute for a Child Care Continuum, Bank Street College of Education.

Porter, T., Rice, R., & Mabon, S. (2003). *Doting on kids: Understanding quality in kith and kin child care.* New York: Institute for a Child Care Continuum, Bank Street College of Education.

Powell, D. R. (1997). Parents' contributions to the quality of child care arrangements. In S. Reifel (Series Ed.) & C. J. Dunst & M. Wolery (Vol. Eds.), *Advances in early education and day care: Vol. 9. Family policy and practice in early child care* (pp. 133–155). Greenwich, CT: JAI Press.

Powell, D. R. (2001). Visions and realities of achieving partnership: Parent–school relationships at the turn of the century. In A. Göncü & E. L. Klein (Eds.), *Children in play, story, and school* (pp. 333–357). New York: Guilford.

Provence, S., Naylor, A., & Patterson, J. (1977). *The challenge of daycare.* New Haven, CT: Yale University Press.

Reschke, K. I., & Walker, S. K. (2005). Grandmothers as child caregivers: A unique child care arrangement. In R. Rice (Ed.), *Perspectives on family, friend and neighbor child care: Research, programs and policy. Occasional paper series* (pp. 33–37). New York: Bank Street College.

Tout, K., & Zaslow, M. (2006). *Observations of child care provided by family, friend and neighbor caregivers in Minnesota.* Minneapolis: Minnesota Child Care Policy Research Partnership. Retrieved January 4, 2007, from http://edocs.dhs.state.mn.us/lfserver/Legacy/DHS-4514-ENG

Vandell, D. L., McCartney, K., Owen, M. T., Booth, C., & Clarke-Stewart, A. (2003). Variations in child care by grandparents during the first three years. *Journal of Marriage and Family, 65,* 375–381.

Zinsser, C. (2001). Child care within the family. *Future of Children, 11,* 123–127.

Chapter 3

Finding and Engaging Family, Friend, and Neighbor Caregivers

*I*n one of the first studies of informal child care, researchers positioned themselves before dawn on streets in working-class neighborhoods of industrial cities in Britain to watch parents and other family members transport and leave their small children in the care of unlicensed providers. The exercise was called a "dawnwatch." It was used to launch an influential study in the early 1970s of informal child care by describing a largely invisible daily routine: "Working parents are tugging their small children through city streets to spend hours in the care of childminders who receive no support, recognition or training for their unbelievably important role in looking after small children" (Jackson & Jackson, 1979, p. 12).

Across the continent several years earlier, two innovative social work researchers in Portland, Oregon, were figuring out how to find and support informal child care. Alice Collins and Eunice Watson eventually discovered that neighborhood social networks could be used to identify child care providers. People in local restaurants, drug stores, and small markets as well as school secretaries, clergy, and public health nurses were particularly helpful in answering the question, "Who does baby sitting around here?" (Collins & Watson, 1969; Galinsky & Hooks, 1977).

The search methods used by these researchers are not standard procedures and certainly would not be appropriate or useful in many neighborhoods and communities. But these novel approaches speak to the problem of how to identify informal child care arrangements. Decades later, the question of how to find family, friend, and neighbor (FFN) caregivers persists in all types of contexts. The largest source of child care for infants and toddlers is not within easy reach of formal systems.

This chapter offers guidelines for finding FFN caregivers. It also describes promising approaches to recruiting informal caregivers for participation in supportive programs and in activities aimed at learning about their interests and needs. These fundamental dimensions of engagement deserve special attention in the development of programs for underserved or never-served populations such as FFN caregivers.

Finding FFN Caregivers

As a general principle, strategies for identifying informal caregivers need to be customized to local circumstances. What works well in one context may be unproductive in another. Search methods need to be crafted in response to a deep understanding of how relationships function and communication flows in a particular setting. Designers of search strategies also need to remember that FFN caregivers are a highly diverse group, as described in chapter 2. There may not be one set of procedures that is equally successful in identifying all subgroups of informal providers. The approaches described below are drawn from a handful of projects designed to support FFN caregivers or to gather information about FFN caregivers. Many of these projects are small-scale or pilot efforts. Our knowledge of how to find FFN caregivers, then, is evolving.

Direct Contact With Caregivers

FFN providers who receive a government child care subsidy are the easiest subgroup of informal caregivers to identify. They are linked to at least one formal child care system and are more likely than some other subgroups of informal providers (e.g., relatives) to see themselves as a caregiver. For example, the FFN care program offered through Georgia's Quality Care for Children program has found participants among caregivers involved in the Child Care Food Program (Runkle, 2006). In this situation, the nutrition program serves as an "on ramp" to the FFN care program.

Finding subsidized caregivers may not be a fully efficient process. Records of caregivers who have received a subsidy may be out of date (e.g., individuals have moved or are no longer providing care). Further, some agencies may track child care subsidy payments by the name and address of the parent, not the caregiver, thereby adding another link in the process of attempting to access caregivers.

Some informal caregivers who receive subsidies—particularly those interested in becoming licensed—no doubt will respond positively to personal and supportive invitations to participate in a child care training offering (see chapter 2). This is an advantageous situation for an agency seeking to support informal caregivers; an existing training resource can be extended to informal providers who are relatively easy to identify. It is not surprising that subsidized FFN providers are typically the primary or sole focus of state initiatives aimed at improving the quality of informal child care (Porter & Kearns, 2005). The major limitation of this arrangement is that informal caregivers who receive a child care subsidy represent an exceptionally small segment of the total FFN population, as described in chapter 2.

To expand the reach of supportive programs for FFN caregivers, experts suggest that efforts should be made to find informal providers through the settings where they "work, pay, play, and pray" (O'Donnell et al., 2006, p. 26). The idea is that workplaces, houses of worship, shopping malls, parks, libraries, apartment building commons rooms, senior citizens centers, and neighborhood stores and restaurants are promising points of access to informal caregivers.

Identifying informal caregivers in a "work, pay, play, or pray" environment is likely to be more complex than placing a notice of an FFN child care project in the church bulletin, for example. The experiences of FFN caregiver support projects suggest that personal contact with familiar, trusted individuals is far superior to the use of impersonal communication channels in finding informal caregivers.

Programs in the Sparking Connections initiative found that working with natural leaders in their respective communities was an effective way to identify and establish a relationship with informal providers. Natural leaders are individuals who are well informed about and respected within a particular setting, often functioning as the "go to" person. They include parents, teachers, service providers, faith leaders, case workers, doulas, public health paraprofessionals, and local business owners. One of the programs affiliated with Sparking Connections tapped well-respected individuals who taught children in local churches to identify and work with informal caregivers (see chapter 4). In another program that wanted to identify FFN providers in a public housing project, housing department staff offered to conduct door-to-door surveys and distribute flyers about the FFN support program. The housing department staff reasoned that they could secure a higher response rate than FFN program staff because the housing staff were familiar to and trusted by housing project residents (O'Donnell et al., 2006).

Although it seems that personal contact is generally superior to impersonal communications, some FFN projects have found printed announcements to be useful in securing participants for focus groups of FFN caregivers. For example, one study distributed fliers advertising a 2-hour discussion for people who are caring for at least one child less than 6 years old for at least 12 hours a week. The flier was distributed throughout the target neighborhood and promised food and child care but did not indicate a $20 stipend would be provided (Porter, 1998).

The use of multiple methods of communication increases the chances of informal caregivers learning about an FFN child care project. For example, coordinators of focus groups for the First 5 California Informal Child Caregiver Support Project used word-of-mouth (e.g., asking caregivers to refer other caregivers); contacted community-based organizations, schools, and health centers; and presented information about focus group sessions at community meetings. In addition to these strategies, the coordinator for caregiver focus groups in a Vietnamese community found that a letter (in Vietnamese) sent to prospective participants was helpful in generating interest in the group. The coordinator for focus groups for a Mien population, which is reportedly difficult to recruit, used announcements on the local Mien radio station plus extensive discussions with community leaders to promote participation in the groups (Drake, Unti, Greenspoon, & Fawcett, 2004).

Indirect Contact Through Families

Another option for finding FFN caregivers is through families. For example, one of the earliest studies of informal caregivers secured its sample by contacting employed mothers through their workplaces. Employers distributed a one-page screening form developed by the researchers for identifying informal child care arrangements. Respondents returned the form in a postage-paid envelope provided by the project, and researchers followed up with an interview when eligibility criteria were met (Emlen, Donoghue, & LaForge, 1971).

More recently, the federally funded Early Head Start initiative designed to support the quality of FFN child care identified caregivers through the families of infants and toddlers enrolled in home-based Early Head Start programs. The first stage of this "follow the child" process was to identify eligible families (enrolled in the home-based option of Early Head Start and use informal child care). The 22 programs participating in the Early Head Start initiative found that having Early Head Start staff identify eligible families was the most successful method. Also helpful were outreach materials such as brochures, posters, and letters to families asking for potential participants in the program. Other strategies for identifying eligible families included referrals from community partners, gathering information about child care arrangements at the point of family enrollment in Early Head Start, and referrals from caregivers participating in the FFN initiative (Paulsell, Mekos, Del Grosso, Banghart, & Nogales, 2006).

Because families are the link to informal caregivers in a "follow the child" approach to identifying FFN providers, the Early Head Start initiative entailed a second stage of informing families of the benefits of the program for their child. This was often done through personal contact with the family, typically with or by the family's usual home visitor from the Early Head Start program. Sometimes the staff would demonstrate to families how educational materials and toys would be a part of the program's work with their child's informal caregiver

(Paulsell et al., 2006). The third stage of recruiting FFN caregivers to the Early Head Start initiative for informal caregivers is described in the next section of this chapter.

The Early Head Start initiative's multimethod approach to identifying informal caregivers did not yield sufficient numbers of participants. The reasons were quite varied: some families had unstable informal child care arrangements; some eligible families left Early Head Start; some families initially eligible for the FFN initiative no longer needed child care; and some families and caregivers were reluctant to enroll in the program. To boost enrollment in the initiative, the participating Early Head Start programs expanded their outreach in several ways—for example, by giving Early Head Start program enrollment priority to waiting list families who were using informal child care (Paulsell et al., 2006).

Recruiting FFN Caregivers

Once FFN caregivers have been identified, the engagement challenge is to respectfully invite and encourage participation in a project related to the quality of FFN child care. This section describes strategies programs have used to promote participation in a support program. This recruitment task usually is more difficult than encouraging participation in a one-time information gathering session such as a telephone interview or focus group. Approaches to engaging caregivers for information-gathering purposes are included in the next section.

The experiences of the Early Head Start program in recruiting caregivers for participation in its FFN child care initiative are informative. Caregivers were approached in one of three ways: Families involved in Early Head Start talked with their child's caregiver about the FFN program; Early Head Start home visitors approached caregivers; or FFN program staff approached caregivers. The program preferred that families initially approach the caregivers because they were "able to vouch for the Early Head Start program and share their positive experiences with the caregivers" (Paulsell et al., 2006, p. 50). FFN program staff members attempted to schedule their initial visit with the caregiver in the caregiver's home because they found that personal contact often was successful in convincing a caregiver to enroll in the program. Program staff also asked families to continue to encourage the caregiver to participate (e.g., talk with the caregiver about the program's benefits).

In the initial meeting with the caregiver, FFN program staff described program services, emphasizing how the program could be helpful to the child and caregiver. Staff also stressed that program services would be tailored to the caregiver's interests and needs, and that participation requirements were flexible. Some staff also tried to engage the child during the visit and demonstrate techniques that the caregiver could use with the child to achieve a developmental goal. For caregivers interested in seeking licensure, staff described how the program could count toward required training hours for licensure. Equipment such as high chairs, gift certificates, books, toys, and other materials available for participation in the program were described as a "selling point" in sites offering these types of items. One staff member reported that she drove a prospective participant to a medical appointment during her first contact with the caregiver to demonstrate how the program could be of logistical help. If a caregiver did not agree to enroll in the program, staff would sometimes approach the caregiver again at a later date (Paulsell et al., 2006).

The initial visit described above includes features that seem essential to encouraging participation in an FFN support program. The introduction to the program was ideally made by a person well known to and trusted by the caregiver. The caregiver's first contact with program staff was personal and individualized. Program staff emphasized the program's benefits for the child while highlighting benefits for the caregiver. Focus group sessions with caregivers who enrolled in the Early Head Start initiative found that they were motivated to participate "for the child's sake"; focus group sessions with parents found that benefits for the caregiver (e.g., someone to talk to, activity ideas, and information) were also a motivation for program participation (Paulsell et al., 2006, p. 51).

The opportunity to receive equipment and materials also appears to be an incentive to participation. Program staff in more than half of the Early Head Start sites indicated that participants' primary motivation for program involvement was access to materials and equipment, followed by support for the caregiver and benefits for the child. The receipt of equipment and materials was cited less frequently by caregivers as a reason for joining the program, however (Paulsell et al., 2006).

In addition to these features, the recruitment experiences of other programs suggest that it is helpful to avoid using technical jargon to describe program services. The task here is to find everyday language that is familiar to the caregiver and provides alternatives to terms such as "training" or "class" (e.g., "a get-together"), "home visit" (e.g., "come by to see you"), and "caregiving" ("when you're watching your grandkid"; see chapter 5). Transportation is important to provide for attendance at program sessions not in easy proximity to the caregiver's residence, and child care also may need to be available if the program session conflicts with the caregiver's responsibilities for children. The provision of food, particularly culturally appropriate meals, is common in group-based programs.

Participation in an individual or group interview (focus group) about informal child care may encourage some persons to join an FFN support program. Even brief discussion of the caregiver role may provide new insights and ideas that enhance the caregiver's commitment to the work, and provide a concrete experiential look at what the program has to offer. Moreover, persons who agree to participate in an information-gathering session are likely to have a keen interest in the topic.

Learning About FFN Caregivers

An essential step in developing an FFN support program is to learn first-hand about the needs and interests of the target population. This information is central to equipping the program with pertinent resources. Chapter 2 offered best guesses about topics of interest to informal caregivers. Local information gathering is critical to due diligence ("know your audience").

Telephone interviews and focus groups are the usual methods for learning about FFN child care for purposes of shaping the design of a caregiver support program. Observations of FFN care have been used infrequently for informing FFN support programs, although this method can be highly useful for learning about FFN care and helping FFN providers reflect on their practices and environments. Other information sources include administrative data collected as part of child care subsidy programs, paper or Web-based questionnaires, community forums, and in-person interviews.

Because different types of methods provide different types of information, program planners often use several methods in a complementary manner. For example, Minnesota's Department of Human Services conducted telephone interviews, focus groups, and observations of FFN care to learn about informal care settings (www.dhs.state.mn.us/main/groups/children/documents/pub/DHS_id_000151.hcsp). The focus groups were used to gather information about child care in refugee and immigrant communities, which is a growing population in Minnesota (Vang, 2006). Planning for an FFN support program in California included focus groups plus interviews with FFN providers who care for children with disabilities and other special needs and with parents of children with disabilities and other special needs (Drake et al., 2004). An Illinois study of license-exempt child care used telephone interviews and administrative data (Anderson, Ramsburg, & Scott, 2005). Promising uses of telephone interviews, focus groups, and observations of FFN care are described below.

Telephone Interviews

Telephone interviews are an efficient way to gather basic information about child care arrangements. Researchers at the Human Services Policy Center at the University of Washington (www.hspc.org) and at the Wilder Foundation in Minnesota (www.wilderresearch.org) are among the growing number of experts with survey experiences focused on FFN child care.

Recently the states of Illinois, Minnesota, and Washington have carried out large-scale surveys of FFN child care, as noted in chapter 1. For example, Minnesota's Department of Human Services, in collaboration with Wilder Research and other partners, conducted a telephone interview with 400 FFN caregivers (Chase, Arnold, Schauben, & Shardlow, 2006) along with the 2004 statewide household child care survey

(Chase, Arnold, Schauben, & Shardlow, 2005). There also was a separate telephone survey with approximately 200 FFN caregivers who were receiving a subsidy through the Minnesota Child Care Assistance Program (Chase, Arnold, & Schauben, 2006).

In addition to securing basic data on characteristics of care arrangements in the statewide sample of 400 FFN providers, the Minnesota researchers gathered information on quality indicators. These included the intentionality of the caregiving (see chapter 2); the extent of caregiver training; the FFN caregiver's connections with other caregivers for information and support; the strength of the caregiver–parent relationship; and the extent of supports for the following developmental domains: literacy, cognitive, social–emotional, and physical development. The self-reported information on these attributes was used to create an index of the quality of care (Chase, Arnold, Schauben, & Shardlow, 2006).

Washington state used telephone interviews with parents and FFN caregivers plus a small number of policymakers and child care advocates to generate an understanding of the scope and needs of FFN child care. The study was conducted by researchers at the Human Services Policy Center at the University of Washington (Brandon, Maher, Joesch, & Doyle, 2002). Many of the interview items in the Washington study were used in the subsequent Minnesota study of FFN care.

The Washington and Minnesota child care surveys used random digit dialing to secure samples of individuals in the general population who cared for other people's children on a regular basis but did not work in centers. For example, the Minnesota researchers purchased random digit samples of listed and unlisted telephone numbers from a survey firm for each region in the state and in the metropolitan area. Each telephone number (more than 29,000) was called in an attempt to secure a sample of FFN providers (a household with one or more adults more than 18 years old who provided FFN care for someone else's children 12 years old or younger at least once a week in each of the prior 2 weeks; Chase, Arnold, Schauben, & Shardlow, 2006). The Washington researchers oversampled in geographic areas with high concentrations of low-income households to ensure an adequate number of low-income respondents (Brandon et al., 2002).

Lists of recipients of child care subsidies are an obvious source for securing a sample of subsidized FFN providers. For example, the Illinois study randomly selected parents from all subsidy recipients using a license-exempt provider at least 15 hours a week. If the parent agreed to be interviewed, then the license-exempt caregiver who provided the most care for that family also was invited to be interviewed. Interviews were completed with 303 pairs of parent and provider, enabling researchers to compare parent and provider perspectives on the same caregiving situations and issues (Anderson et al., 2005). Specific counties were targeted in the Minnesota study of subsidized FFN child care (Chase, Arnold, & Schauben, 2006).

Listed and unlisted telephone numbers of a general population are commonly used in survey research on a variety of topics. Currently this sampling approach systematically omits families and providers who do not maintain a land phone (that is, have no telephone or maintain a cell phone exclusively). Survey participants, then, may not be fully representative of all population subgroups. This problem would not occur with updated child care subsidy lists for which participants have provided their contact data. However, information secured from partici- pants in child care subsidy programs is useful in thinking primarily about subsidized child care and cannot be generalized to FFN arrange- ments that are not receiving subsidies.

Focus Groups

Designers of FFN support programs often have used focus groups to gather information from providers and parents. Focus groups may pro- vide more detailed, nuanced perspectives on FFN care than structured interviews. The experiences of some researchers suggest that low-income women in particular are more comfortable sharing information in the context of a peer group discussion than in a one-to-one interview (e.g., Porter, 1998). One well-regarded resource on how to conduct focus groups is *Focus Groups: A Practical Guide for Applied Research* (Krueger & Casey, 2000).

Illustrations of the use of focus groups to learn about FFN arrange- ments include studies by Toni Porter and colleagues at Bank Street College's Institute for a Child Care Continuum (www.bnkst.edu/iccc/).

The Institute's first focus group study identified challenges faced by kith and kin caregivers and the kinds of support they wanted (Porter, 1998, 1999). More recently, Porter and colleagues conducted focus groups to learn about caregivers' perceptions of the quality in FFN arrangements (Porter et al., 2003). This information was used to develop measures of FFN quality (see below).

Focus groups were part of an information-gathering strategy used to develop the First 5 California Informal Child Caregiver Support Project. Persons were recruited for the focus groups by individuals from the same language background as prospective participants. The intent was to ensure that members of targeted communities were recruited. In recruiting focus group participants, staff found that it was helpful to describe the importance of the project, to emphasize the opportunity for caregivers to provide input into the design of the support project, and to talk about incentives for participation (e.g., children's books, puppets, or $30 gift certificate to a store). The organizer of the caregiver focus groups in a Vietnamese community in the California project found that a letter (in Vietnamese) sent to prospective participants was helpful in generating interest in the group. Arranging for transportation and child care were among the challenges encountered by coordinators in recruiting focus group participants (Drake et al., 2004).

Observations

Systematic observations of an FFN setting typically provide more reliable information on the quality of care than self-reported information because persons involved in the arrangement are likely to have inherent biases. Observational work is time intensive, in part because establishing the reliability of observers requires considerable training and monitoring.

Minnesota's observational study of FFN child care was conducted to complement findings from the telephone surveys described above. The intent of the observational work was to provide snapshots of caregiver–child interactions, the provision of learning opportunities, materials and activities, space and equipment, and health and safety provisions. The sample consisted of 41 caregivers identified through the larger FFN surveys. Each was observed engaged in caregiving activities in their home for 2½ hours by trained data collectors using measurement tools adapted from a national study of child care. FFN providers in the sample were more oriented to FFN caregiving as a profession than the average respondent in the survey samples (Tout & Zaslow, 2006). Findings of this study, which are summarized in the previous section of this chapter, were used to formulate recommendations on needed supports for FFN child care.

Concerns have been raised about the appropriateness of assessing the quality of FFN care with tools used to measure quality in licensed or regulated family child care homes, as noted in chapter 1. To address this situation, the Institute for a Child Care Continuum at Bank Street College of Education is developing instruments to assess the quality of care provided by relatives, friends, and neighbors. To date, work has been done on a version for relative care. The Child Care Assessment Tool for Relatives (CCAT-R) focuses on the quality of relative care provided for children younger than 6 years old. An intended use of the instrument is to identify areas in need of attention in program development or training efforts (Porter, Rice, & Rivera, 2006).

The CCAT-R, which requires 2½ to 3 hours of observation time, measures the frequency of caregiver and child interactions that support language, cognitive, physical, and socioemotional development; health and safety (food preparation, environment, routines, outdoor play); and the availability of materials that support child development (e.g., crayons, rattles, books, balls, and riding toys). The tool also includes an interview with the caregiver that includes attention to attitudes toward child care, relationships with parents, and how the caregiver balances child care with home life.

The CCAT-R was developed through consultations with child care researchers and practitioners, reviews of existing measures of child care quality, focus groups with caregivers, and field testing with an ethnically and geographically diverse group of 92 relative caregivers. Future work with this measure will provide additional information on its reliability and validity (Porter et al., 2006).

Participants in focus groups, many interview studies, and observation studies are unlikely to be representative of the larger population of FFN caregivers. Because all informal providers in the highly invisible and diverse sector of FFN care cannot be readily identified, it is impossible to systematically select a representative group of caregivers from a larger population of informal caregivers. Results, then, cannot be generalized to a larger population, but the information secured from volunteers in an information-gathering method may well represent the interests and needs of volunteers for an FFN support program.

In sum, this chapter reviews a number of methods for finding and learning about FFN caregivers, arguably among the biggest challenges in developing a program of support to informal child care. The chapter's focus on engagement strategies is a companion to the content focus of chapter 2, which offered some best guesses on information and resources of interest to FFN caregivers as well as meaningful ways in which FFN providers differ from one another. Together, these chapters provide a road map for program developers to establish a foundation for promoting quality in FFN child care, the topic of the next chapter.

References

Anderson, S. G., Ramsburg, D. M., & Scott, J. (2005). *Illinois study of license-exempt child care: Final report.* Springfield, IL: Illinois Department of Human Services.

Brandon, R. N., Maher, E. J., Joesch, J. M., & Doyle, S. (2002). *Understanding family, friend, and neighbor care in Washington state: Developing appropriate training and support.* Seattle: Human Services Policy Center, Evans School of Public Affairs, University of Washington.

Chase, R., Arnold, J., & Schauben, L. (2006). *Family, friends and neighbors caring for children through the Minnesota Child Care Assistance Program.* St. Paul, MN: Wilder Research. Retrieved November 3, 2006, from http://edocs.dhs.state.mn.us/lfserver/Legacy/DHS-4517-ENG

Chase, R., Arnold, J., Schauben, L., & Shardlow, B. (2005). *Child care use in Minnesota: 2004 statewide household child care survey.* St. Paul, MN: Wilder Research. Retrieved November 3, 2006, from http://edocs.dhs.state.mn.us/lfserver/Legacy/DHS-4623-ENG

Chase, R., Arnold, J., Schauben, L., & Shardlow, B. (2006). *Family, friend and neighbor caregivers: Results of the 2004 Minnesota statewide household child care survey.* St. Paul, MN: Wilder Research. Retrieved November 3, 2006, from http://edocs.dhs.state.mn.us/lfserver/Legacy/DHS-4516-ENG

Collins, A., & Watson, E. (1969). *The day care neighbor service.* Portland, OR: Tri-County Community Council.

Drake, P. J., Unti, L., Greenspoon, B., & Fawcett, L. K. (2004). *First Five California informal child caregiver support project: Focus groups and interviews report.* Sacramento, CA: First 5 California Children and Families Commission and ETS Associates.

Emlen, A. C., Donoghue, B. A., & LaForge, R. (1971). *Child care by kith: A study of the family day care relationships of working mothers and neighborhood caregivers.* Report to the Extramural Research and Demonstration Grants Branch, Children's Bureau, U.S. Department of Health, Education, and Welfare. Portland, OR: Tri-County Community Council and Portland State University.

Galinsky, E., & Hooks, W. H. (1977). *The new extended family: Day care that works.* Boston: Houghton Mifflin.

Jackson, B., & Jackson, S. (1979). *Childminder.* Boston: Routledge & Kegan Paul.

Krueger R. A., & Casey, M. A. (2000). *Focus groups: A practical guide for applied research* (3rd ed.). Thousand Oaks, CA: Sage.

O'Donnell, N. S., Cochran, M., Lekies, K., Diehl, D., Morrissey, T. W., Ashley, N., et al. (2006). *Sparking Connections, Phase II: A multi-site evaluation of community-based strategies to support family, friend and neighbor caregivers of children. Part 1: Lessons learned and recommendations.* New York: Families and Work Institute.

Paulsell, D., Mekos, D., Del Grosso, P., Banghart, P., & Nogales, R. (2006). *The Enhanced Home Visiting Pilot Project: How Early Head Start programs are reaching out to kith and kin caregivers.* Final interim report submitted to the U.S. Department of Health and Human Services, Administration of Children, Youth and Families, Head Start Bureau. Princeton, NJ: Mathematica Policy Research.

Porter, T. (1998). *Neighborhood child care: Family, friends and neighbors talk about caring for other people's children.* New York: Center for Family Support, Bank Street College of Education.

Porter, T. (1999). Infants and toddlers in kith and kin care: Findings from the informal care project. *Zero to Three, 19,* 27–35.

Porter, T., & Kearns, S. M. (2005). *Supporting family, friend and neighbor caregivers: Findings from a survey of state policies.* New York: Institute for a Child Care Continuum, Bank Street College of Education.

Porter, T., Rice, R., & Rivera, E. (2006). *Assessing quality in family, friend and neighbor care: The child care assessment tool for relatives.* New York: Institute for a Child Care Continuum, Bank Street College of Education.

Runkle, P. (2006, November). *Promising practices for family, friend and neighbor child care.* Panel presentation at the annual meeting of the National Alliance for Family, Friend and Neighbor Child Care, Atlanta, GA.

Tout, K., & Zaslow, M. (2006). *Observations of child care provided by family, friend and neighbor caregivers in Minnesota.* Minneapolis: Minnesota Child Care Policy Research Partnership. Retrieved January 5, 2007, from http://edocs.dhs.state.mn.us/lfserver/Legacy/DHS-4514-ENG

Vang, C. Y. (2006). *Family, friend and neighbor child care providers in recent immigrant and refugee communities.* St. Paul: Minnesota Department of Human Services. Retrieved January 5, 2007, from http://edocs.dhs.state.mn.us/lfserver/Legacy/DHS-4518-ENG

Chapter 4

Promoting Quality in Family, Friend, and Neighbor Care

What types of support are available for helping family members, friends, and neighbors (FFN) improve the quality of their caregiving practices? How should support be provided? And who should offer assistance? Guidelines for answering these questions are offered in this chapter. The intent is to suggest a menu of options for crafting the design of a program in response to the needs and interests of FFN caregivers.

Types of Support

Expert information on how to promote the healthy development of infants and toddlers is readily accessible in a growing number of sources. In addition to publications such as those available through ZERO TO THREE Press, there are credible Internet resources such as the Tufts University's Child & Family WebGuide (http://cfs.tufts.edu). There also are user-friendly syntheses and summaries of research on environments and practices that support positive well-being in the early years in a range of domains such as literacy and language development (e.g., Bardige, 2005; Rosenkoetter & Knapp-Philo, 2006). Safety equipment and children's toys and books may be secured at reduced cost from retailers and perhaps at no cost from charitable organizations.

It is efficient to use an existing training program or curriculum versus pursuing the costly task of creating a curriculum from scratch when an available resource can be closely aligned to the interests and needs of FFN caregivers targeted by a program. Some examples of curriculum resources are described below. Although these resources focus on infants and toddlers, children in the care of some FFN providers span a wide age range, as noted in chapter 2. This means that some caregivers may want a program that addresses more than infant and toddler content (see chapter 5).

Curriculum Examples

Because supportive programs for FFN caregivers are relatively new, curricula originally developed for parents and/or child care providers have been extended to FFN populations by many programs. Examples are described below.

Promoting First Relationships (PFR; www.son.washington.edu/centers/pfr/) is a curriculum developed by the University of Washington's Department of Child and Family Nursing for service providers to help parents and other caregivers meet young children's social and emotional needs. It has been implemented with low-income English- and Spanish-speaking individuals in culturally diverse communities who care for infants and toddlers. This effort was supported by a grant from the Annie E. Casey Foundation and carried out in collaboration with the Human Services Policy Center at the University of Washington. An evaluation of the program found positive changes in grandmothers' overall caregiving skills, including sensitivity to cues, response to distress, and fostering of social–emotional and cognitive growth. There also was a significant decrease in grandmothers' depression. Grandmothers were enrolled in either an 8-week home visiting program or an 8-week group program, both based on the PFR curriculum. There were no significant differences between the groups regarding positive effects of the program (Maher & Kelly, 2007).

Curriculum content includes attention to foundations of social and emotional development from birth to 3 years old; elements of a healthy relationship, including trust and security; understanding and intervening with children's challenging behaviors; and consultation strategies for working with parents and other caregivers. PFR has been used with child care providers, Early Head Start staff, families in a transitional housing program, homeless families, and foster care caregivers.

The **Supporting Care Providers** curriculum developed by the Parents as Teachers National Center (PATNC; www.patnc.org) for child care providers, including FFN caregivers, is an outgrowth of PATNC's Born to Learn parent education curriculum. Supporting Care Providers is delivered through personal visits to providers. Topics include child development, emerging reading and writing, environments, observation of children, brain development, partnerships with families, safety and health, sensory experiences, and school readiness. The curriculum guide for trainers includes personal visit plans; handouts for both providers and parents; and sections on appropriate toys and materials, songs and rhymes, stories, and special topics such as divorce, understanding death, and biting. The curriculum has been used extensively in Missouri, the home of PATNC, and beyond, including several initiatives described in the "How Support Is Offered" section of this chapter.

Working With Home-Based Caregivers: A Guide for Trainers was developed by the Institute for a Child Care Continuum at Bank Street College (www.bankstreet.edu/ICCC/) for staff who work with legally exempt and regulated home-based child care providers. The training includes modules on parent–caregiver communication; language and literacy, including bilingual language development; numeracy; discipline; caregiver–child interaction activities; health, safety, and nutrition; community resources; and trainer competencies regarding group facilitation and understanding adult learners. The child development content extends beyond the first 3 years of life. The training has been conducted for numerous programs aimed at supporting FFN child care, including the projects described in this chapter.

The **Program for Infant/Toddler Care** (PITC; www.pitc.org), developed through a collaboration of the California Department of Education and WestEd, is a relationship-based curriculum aimed at helping caregivers get "in tune" with what each infant needs, thinks, and feels. PITC emphasizes relationship (vs. lesson) planning and child-directed (vs. adult-directed) learning. The curriculum promotes primary care, small groups, continuity, individualized care, cultural responsiveness, and inclusion of children with special needs. In addition to responsiveness to each infant's eagerness to learn, the program helps caregivers create safe and developmentally challenging environments, and strengthen the child's developing family and cultural identity through meaningful connections with each child's family and culture.

PITC training materials include videos, guides, and manuals. The program is the basis of training for infant and toddler caregivers throughout California and in numerous other states and several foreign countries. It has been a major source of training for Early Head Start staff nationally. The program has been extended to FFN populations in several locations.

Equipment and Materials

Safety equipment and materials to help children learn are commonly provided by FFN support programs, and were recognized as an incentive to participation in an FFN support program in chapter 3's description of approaches to recruiting caregivers. Surveys consistently show that many informal caregivers need and desire items related to quality child care. In the Washington state survey, for example, informal caregivers expressed interest in activity boxes, toys, and play kits that provide age-appropriate activities for caregivers to use with children (35%), and home safety kits such as child-proof latches, covers for electrical outlets, and smoke and fire detection equipment (35%; Brandon, Maher, Joesch, & Doyle, 2002).

Recognition of Caregiver Role

Programs that work with FFN caregivers have found that some caregivers are socially isolated (e.g., O'Donnell et al., 2006), and many caregivers feel that their special relationship with the children in their care is underappreciated or unappreciated (Porter et al., 2003). Participants in FFN support programs often note that a benefit of the program is recognition of their contributions to a child's development (see chapter 5). It is not clear what features or components of a program provide affirmation of caregivers' importance. Most likely it is a combination of program attributes, including the quality of relationships and the provision of suggestions in nonjudgmental ways.

How Support Is Offered

The way in which support is provided to FFN caregivers is as important as the substance of the assistance. Some basics here include use of the language of the caregiver, staff who communicate a genuine commitment to improving the well-being of infants and toddlers and their caregivers, mutually reciprocal relationships with caregivers and all others in their settings, and respectful recognition of the ways in which caregivers learn and receive help. With regard to this latter point, it is important to note that some surveys have found that many FFN caregivers have had limited formal education (Brandon et al., 2002) and little or no experience with formal training programs (Anderson, Ramsburg, & Scott, 2005). In general, there is a tendency to tap informal sources of assistance (others friends and relatives) for support in the caregiver role (Chase, Arnold, Schauben, & Shardlow, 2006) and, as noted earlier, to not see themselves as a caregiver or child care provider.

A range of methods has been implemented with some success by FFN support programs. Studies conducted to date have not identified a "silver bullet" or superior approach to working with informal caregivers. Each method has distinctive characteristics. For example, group approaches can provide peer support for the caregiver role, whereas home visits provide a unique opportunity to individualize work with the caregiver. Individuals differ in their preferences for the way in which they receive help. For example, the study of the Promoting First Relationships program (previously described) found home visits and group sessions appealed to a different subset of grandmothers based on their personalities and life circumstances (Maher & Kelly, 2007).

One-to-one formats. Home visits and other forms of one-to-one contact have a long history in the parenting education and family support field (e.g., Powell, 2006) and are now used to support FFN caregivers. The Cherokee Nation Sparking Connections Program in Oklahoma, for example, used monthly home visits over a 12-month period to reach relative providers. The visits were conducted by a child care resource educator who used the Supporting Care Providers curriculum developed by the National Center for Parents as Teachers (described above). The program provided incentives of a small stipend plus a certificate of completion for each of four goal areas: health and safety, school readiness skills, Cherokee language and culture, and learning opportunities. In a survey completed at the end of the program, participants pointed to benefits and growth in each of the goal areas (e.g., CPR skills, realistic expectations of children; Caudill, 2005).

Surveys of FFN caregivers have found that a sizeable group of providers would like an expert to call when questions or concerns arise. In the Washington state survey described in chapter 3, for example, 33% of respondents indicated they would like a resource line, and 10% expressed interest in an in-home visit to help with a particular child (Brandon et al., 2002).

Group formats. Group formats are a common system for providing information and social support. There is a range of possibilities, from interactive workshops to formal presentations by an expert that include a question and answer component. Group formats also include support groups that consist primarily of open-ended discussion of topics of interest to group participants.

Some programs combine presentations by an expert with elements of a support or discussion group approach. For example, the Arizona Kith and Kin Project developed by the Association for Supportive Child Care provides regular group sessions that feature a child care topic such as guidance and discipline, nutrition, parent–caregiver relationships, language and literacy, brain development, and topics requested by group members. Sessions typically include a sharing time for discussion of the session's topic or a topic of interest to participants. The weekly sessions, often conducted in Spanish, run for 2 hours each across 14 weeks. Group size ranges from a minimum of 6 to a maximum of 20 participants (www.asccaz.gov; Ocampo-Schlesinger & McCarty, 2005).

A qualitative follow-up study of program "graduates" conducted by an external evaluator found that some former participants (all Spanish speaking) were still in communication with participants and leaders some several years after their original groups had ceased to meet. They attributed to the program a better understanding of children's developmental stages and age-appropriate behavior, and a more positive approach to discipline in their caregiving. They spoke of being more patient and tolerant, and of being more knowledgeable of activities that support children's learning and of nutrition and first aid practices (Ocampo-Schlesinger & McCarty, 2005; Welch, 2002).

Some group formats include both children and their caregivers. A prominent example is the Play and Learn program implemented in a number of locations, including Seattle/King County, Washington; Georgia; Minnesota; and Hawaii. At a typical Play and Learn group, a facilitator leads children's art and craft activities. A circle time features shared book reading, songs, finger play, and music and movement. There also is an opportunity for children to engage in free play with toys provided by the program and to socialize with peers and other adults (Steinke, 2006).

The guideline of accessing caregivers through community-based settings, emphasized in chapter 3, also applies to the location of group meetings and other services. Mosques and commons rooms of apartment building complexes in the target population's neighborhood are examples of settings that programs have found to be psychologically as well as logistically accessible to participants.

Newsletters, booklets, and videos. Surveys of FFN providers have found strong interest in receiving videos, books, booklets, tip sheets, and newsletters related to the care of young children, perhaps because this is a convenient way to access information (Anderson et al., 2005; Brandon et al., 2002). The Cornell University Early Childhood Program has developed a series of newsletters in collaboration with the New York State Office of Children and Family Services. The contents of the newsletter are based on results of focus groups with providers. Newsletters are available in English and in Spanish, and address topics such as parent–provider communication, infants and toddlers, helping children learn to love reading, keeping children safe and healthy, and caring for relatives (www.human.cornell.edu/HD/CECP/).

Mobile vans. Mobile vans that contain toy and book lending libraries have been used with success in several states, particularly states with large rural counties, and cities. In Georgia's Quality Care for Children initiative for FFN caregivers, for example, a resource and lending van is equipped with toys, equipment, educational tapes, videos, and publications that can be used to enhance the learning environment of FFN settings. The resource van brings items to the home of informal caregivers

(Runkle, 2006). The Seattle/King County, Washington, program associated with the Sparking Connections initiative prepared "Ready, Set, Go" bags of children's books, toys, library card applications, and child care tips that are distributed to FFN caregivers through retailers such as local grocers (O'Donnell et al., 2006).

Multimethod approaches. Support programs for FFN providers often provide more than one way for participants to be involved, usually in an attempt to increase the intensity of a program and to complement the unique features of each method (e.g., peer support in a group, individualized attention in a home visit). It is common for one-to-one formats to be combined with other methods. The Cherokee Nation program (described earlier) provided network meetings once a month that included a content focus (e.g., first aid) as well as a time to share ideas and socialize with other relative providers. The program also provided health and safety items to providers who needed them (Caudill, 2005). Attendance at the monthly network meetings was minimal initially but steadily grew as caregivers became familiar with the format and offerings (O'Donnell et al., 2006).

The Caring for Quality Project in Rochester, New York, also provides home visits and networking meetings in an effort to increase the quality of care provided to young children in both registered and informal (license exempt) family child care homes. Networking meetings are facilitated by the home visitors and occur monthly with small groups of no more than seven providers. An evaluation of the program by the Cornell University Early Childhood Program found that the quality of the family child care programs increased when providers participated in the project. Nearly three quarters of the providers who were rated as being more engaged in the program by their home visitors showed increases in quality, whereas fewer than one half of providers rated as less engaged in the program showed an increase in quality over time. Home visitor observations also pointed to positive program impact (e.g., a caregiver "learned the importance of actually playing with the children and doing hands on projects with them"; www.human.cornell.edu/HD/CECP/).

The Early Head Start initiative for informal caregivers is distinctive in its inclusion of all adults who have responsibility for the target child's care. This includes the child's parent or parents plus the FFN provider. This enables the program to address a goal of increasing the consistency of care across home and child care settings as well as other goals related to the informal arrangement (e.g., improve parent–caregiver relationships). In addition to regular home visits, the initiative also provided home safety items and children's books and toys plus support groups (Paulsell, Mekos, Del Grosso, Banghart, & Nogales, 2006).

Who Provides Support

The characteristics and accommodations of the agencies and the staff who work with FFN caregivers are key considerations in developing an FFN support program. Guidelines for each of these areas are offered below.

Agency Platforms and Accommodations

In the early steps of developing a program of support to FFN caregivers, it is important to take stock of the capacity of an agency regarding its potential helpfulness to informal child care providers. This requires a careful look at an agency's platform in relation to the needs and interests of FFN providers. The question here is how an agency's expertise, existing relations with FFN providers, mission, and ways of behaving can be marshaled to serve FFN caregivers. For example, some organizations have a long history of using home visits to serve their target population, whereas other agencies have extensive expertise in conducting support groups or classroom-style trainings. How well does an existing strength of an agency map on to the needs and interests of FFN caregivers?

In reaching out to FFN caregivers, agencies are likely to extend what they already know and do well. For example, most programs involved in an Early Head Start initiative for FFN caregivers used their well-developed approach to home visits with families as the model for providing services to informal caregivers (Paulsell et al., 2006). The extent to which an agency sees children, families, or child care providers as its primary constituency also is likely to influence the organizational posture toward FFN caregivers. Consider, for instance, the actions of a child care resource and referral (CCR&R) agency with a plentiful supply of baby cribs in storage. Agency leaders opted to not loan the cribs to participants in a training program the agency offered to FFN caregivers. In the eyes of agency officials, the cribs were to be distributed as a reward to providers who achieved licensed status. Apparently licensed providers were this agency's primary constituency.

Put simply, an agency needs to determine whether its customary ways of thinking about and serving others are also a promising approach to supporting FFN caregivers. Organizations may need to move out of their "comfort zone" to provide meaningful support to caregivers in informal child care arrangements.

Two types of agencies commonly cited as appropriate organizations for supporting FFN caregivers are described in the next section in terms of typical capacities and challenges. The organizations are agencies that offer child care provider training and agencies that provide parenting education and family support services. Although mentioned less frequently, community-based health organizations are another potential platform for reaching FFN providers. For example, doulas (experienced women who help other women around the time of childbirth) have a rich history of providing family support (Abramson, Breedlove, & Isaacs, 2006), and public health nurses have proven to be effective in improving the outcomes of first-time mothers and their children (Olds et al., 2002).

Agencies that offer child care provider training. Organizations that offer child care provider training and technical assistance such as CCR&R agencies are widely viewed as appropriate systems of support for FFN caregivers.

Agency strengths include recognized expertise in the care of young children and established mechanisms for delivering training and assistance to child care providers.

At the same time, agencies that offer child care provider training often face several challenges in extending their resources to FFN populations, especially to caregivers who do not aspire to become a licensed provider (see chapter 2).

One challenge is to ensure that the organizational mission sufficiently embraces support to unlicensed providers. Generally a primary goal of conventional sources of child care provider training is to improve the quality of child care through licensure. Agencies that provide child care training often function as influential advocates for strengthening the training requirements for securing and maintaining licensure, and they oppose policies that leave the task of monitoring the quality of child care in the hands of parent consumers alone. Obviously this mission runs contrary to key attributes of FFN child care (see chapter 5).

A related challenge is to fully support the policy of offering subsidies to eligible children in the care of FFN providers. This subsidy, which cumulatively represents substantial sums of money in most states, can be viewed as an inappropriate diversion of resources from licensed providers, with minimal or no accountability regarding standards of care. Critics have argued, for example, that public support of FFN care implies that "the training we've already determined is crucial to the child's experience is irrelevant" and has the effect of undermining "higher pay and benefits for child care teachers by flooding the market with untrained cheap labor" (Gordon, 2000, p. 33).

In addition, the organizational capacity to reach and serve FFN caregivers may need to be strengthened. It is unlikely that there are existing ties between FFN caregivers and agencies that primarily serve child care providers who are licensed, wish to become licensed, or work in licensed facilities.

Agencies that offer family and parenting education and support.
Another organizational platform for supporting FFN caregivers is agencies that provide family and parenting education and support. Some agencies that provide family support also work directly with the child (e.g., Early Head Start). Organizations that offer family and parenting education may be a particularly appealing resource for FFN child care providers who approach their caregiver role as an extension of parenting.

Organizational strengths include content expertise in family relationships that may be highly applicable to many FFN child care settings plus direct links to families through established systems of community outreach. Some participants in a parenting program are likely to be FFN caregivers. Agencies that provide family and parenting programs also may encounter several challenges in attempts to serve FFN caregivers.

One challenge is accessibility. Some programs of family and parenting education and support are limited to parents or grandparents. This restriction poses obvious problems for agencies seeking to serve more than the grandparent segment of the FFN caregiver population. A related problem is that some communities may not have an ongoing organizational source of family and parenting education or may have a parenting program that exclusively serves populations deemed to be at risk for abusing or neglecting their children.

Another challenge is to adjust the family and parenting education content to accommodate the interests and needs of FFN caregivers. Program content that focuses heavily on parent development or family relationships, for example, may provide insufficient attention to child development and care practices that promote children's growth and development.

Agency accommodations. Most agencies that seek to serve FFN caregivers are likely to make or need accommodations in existing areas of content expertise and methods of serving their usual population group. The changes range from adapting customary approaches to acquiring fully new content and methods of working with others, including agency partners.

Mission statements may need to be revised. Examples include reworking the mission statement of a CCR&R agency to focus on all children regardless of care arrangement or on all child care providers regardless of licensure status or intent (see chapter 5), and changing the mission of a parenting education organization to fully serve more than biological or adoptive parents. Of course, revision of an agency's mission statement is a hollow act without a corresponding change in the agency's practices and programs as well as the beliefs and behaviors of its members, from staff to board members and volunteers. This may be a time-consuming process if there is strong resistance to serving FFN caregivers.

Responsive support of FFN providers affords an agency with the opportunity to adapt existing training programs or adopt new resources. For example, it appears that informal caregivers face unique challenges in maintaining positive relations with parents (see chapter 2) that existing resources related to this topic (focused on licensed facilities, including centers) would not fully address. More generally, programs aimed at improving the quality of FFN care give less attention to helping caregivers negotiate and maintain productive partnerships with parents than to the usual child care topics of health, safety, and child development (Porter & Kearns, 2005). Expansion of an agency's portfolio of curricula or program resources may mean, for instance, that a CCR&R agency adopts an FFN-appropriate curriculum generated in a parenting education context (e.g., the Supporting Care Providers program developed by the National Center for Parents as Teachers). For existing staff of an agency, successfully embracing new modes for delivering a program may be a more challenging task than acquiring new content expertise. The skill sets required for conducting effective home visits and group sessions are not fully interchangeable, for example.

Agency collaborations. Collaborations with other organizations are a common way for agencies to complement their existing capacity for serving FFN providers. Nearly one half of the programs involved in the Early Head Start FFN initiative, for example, collaborated with a CCR&R agency. The CCR&R often provided group training for caregivers and sometimes offered access to lending libraries of toys and children's books. CCR&R agencies were not productive sources of referral to informal providers in the Early Head Start FFN initiative, however. Early Head Start programs also partnered with family support and home visiting programs, health care providers, programs serving young children with special needs, family literacy programs, mental health and social services agencies, the local Cooperative Extension Service, public schools, libraries, and a juvenile corrections department, among others (Paulsell et al., 2006).

The Early Head Start programs used an informal process for identifying and inviting community partners to be involved in the FFN initiative. Most programs selected community partners with whom they had an existing relationship (e.g., part of same umbrella organization or history of collaboration on other efforts). Evaluators of the Early Head Start FFN effort determined that two thirds of the partnerships across the

23 programs were strong or evolving. Strong partnerships had a shared vision and clearly defined roles at an early point in the FFN effort, and evolving partnerships were moving in the direction of strengthening existing collaborations, sometimes by disbanding ineffective ones. One third of programs had less success with partnerships for the FFN effort; in most cases, collaboration plans had not been implemented at the time of evaluator site visits due to challenges of commitment and coordination (Paulsell et al., 2006).

Partnership experiences in the Early Head Start FFN initiative are a reminder of the time required to carefully craft new collaborations or rework prior or existing partnerships. Clear communication about roles and expectations early in the process is one of the essential elements of building a solid partnership. For example, a partner in one of the Early Head Start sites was frustrated because the agency knew of many grandparents raising grandchildren but was unable to enroll them in the Early Head Start FFN initiative because the child (grandchild) was not enrolled in Early Head Start (Paulsell et al., 2006).

Program Staff

Probably it is an understatement to submit that staff responsibilities in FFN support programs are among the most challenging of all work in the human and educational services. This is an assignment for highly resourceful individuals who bring expertise in infant and toddler development, demonstrated competence in high-quality child care practices, a passionate commitment to improving the well-being of very young children, and interpersonal savvy to a multitude of tasks. As a starting point, staff need to appreciate a program context in which "clients" do not seek out professional or agency services.

Some programs of support to FFN caregivers have responded to the complexities of the work by finding and recruiting individuals who are respected members of the community or setting the program seeks to serve. One of the first FFN support programs pursued this strategy. The Day Care Neighbor Services project, established in the late 1960s in Portland, Oregon (see chapter 3), identified community residents for leadership positions as day care neighbors. These individuals already were at the center of a natural helping system in the neighborhood in that they were routinely approached by residents with questions or concerns about children. The Day Care Neighbor Services project sought to enhance this role by providing periodic consultation with the day care neighbors (Collins & Watson, 1969). This approach is generally consistent with this volume's guidance about the use of respected leaders in a community for finding FFN caregivers in culturally responsive ways (see chapter 3).

At the same time, some agencies have staffed FFN support programs with individuals who hold undergraduate or advanced degrees in child development, early education, social work, or a closely related field. This was the staffing pattern in the Early Head Start FFN initiative, where a majority of home visitors had an associate's or bachelor's degree in a human services or education field and two thirds had prior experience working in Early Head Start or Head Start. The Early Head Start program supervisors also looked for staff who were flexible, per-sistent, and "not easily flustered by what they might encounter in caregivers' homes" (Paulsell et al., 2006, p. 23). Some directors also emphasized the importance of hiring staff who would be viewed by caregivers as a peer, such as a grandmother or someone with similar life experiences (Paulsell et al., 2006).

The emerging area of support programs for FFN caregivers has yet to generate a research base to guide staffing decisions. Until evidence is available, decision makers may find it helpful to consider the research literature on uses of professionals versus paraprofessionals in parenting education and family support programs. The evidence suggests that nurses were more effective than paraprofessionals in delivering a home-based intervention with first-time mothers with high-risk backgrounds (Olds et al., 2002), and that paraprofessionals have an important role to assume in a staffing mix that includes experienced professionals as well as ongoing in-service training supports (Musick & Stott, 2000).

Community Awareness Strategies

In addition to directly providing information and support to FFN care-givers, several agencies have developed strategies aimed at increasing community awareness of the importance of FFN care. This approach was pursued by the SOAR Opportunity Fund in King County (Seattle), Washington in partnership with Sparking Connections (O'Donnell et al., 2006). The Opportunity Fund and its grantees (six community-based agencies) sought to raise community awareness on the following primary message: "Family, friend and neighbor caregivers have an important role in contributing to children's development, school readiness, and success in school." Secondary messages focused on the advantages of FFN care to parents and children, including maintaining their culture; the high percentage of children in FFN care; the important role of parents in encouraging FFN caregivers to support their children's development; and community support for FFN caregivers will help create good outcomes for children and families (Organizational Research Services, 2005, p. 30).

The main forms of community awareness activities were one-on-one meetings and e-mail messages. The countywide CCR&R agency established an electronic mailing list, known as the FFN Roundtable, to provide a forum for organizations interested in FFN child care to share resources, address issues, and provide guidance on strengthening support for FFN care in King County. More than 130 individuals from various organizations, including local government units, were members of the list as of March 2005 (Organizational Research Services, 2005).

Participating agency records indicated that more than 5,000 individuals were reached through the King County community awareness efforts, particularly parents and caregivers. The messages actually conveyed emphasizes the importance of supporting FFN caregivers, resources available to support FFN care, and defining or clarifying the "FFN" term. Intended messages regarding the parent's role in supporting FFN care and the advantages and prevalence of FFN care were infrequently conveyed. There were differences across the six participating agencies in which messages were emphasized. For example, organizations that were new to FFN activities tended to focus more on defining FFN child care, whereas messages conveyed by the CCR&R tended to focus on the community's role in supporting FFN care. Interviews with 30 individuals who had been contacted for community awareness purposes plus an on-line survey of the electronic mailing list (FFN Roundtable) members found that nearly 75% changed what they knew about FFN care through their contacts with the agencies. However, nearly one quarter of interviewees were unfamiliar with FFN care at the time of the interview though they were members of organizations that received information about FFN care as part of the community awareness strategies. Among the vast majority with heightened awareness of FFN care, there were increases in knowledge about resources and support for FFN child care and the prevalence, advantages, and importance of FFN care (Organizational Research Services, 2005).

References

Abramson, R., Breedlove, G. K., & Isaacs, B. (2006). *The community-based doula: Supporting families before, during, and after childbirth.* Washington, DC: ZERO TO THREE.

Anderson, S. G., Ramsburg, D. M., & Scott, J. (2005). *Illinois study of license-exempt child care: Final report.* Springfield, IL: Illinois Department of Human Services.

Bardige, B. (2005). *At a loss for words: How America is failing our children and what we can do about it.* Philadelphia: Temple University Press.

Brandon, R. N., Maher, E. J., Joesch, J. M., & Doyle, S. (2002). *Understanding family, friend, and neighbor care in Washington state: Developing appropriate training and support.* Seattle: Human Services Policy Center, Evans School of Public Affairs, University of Washington.

Caudill, D. (2005). *Report on outcomes of Cherokee Nation Sparking Connections Program.* Tahlequah, OK: Cherokee Nation. Retrieved January 5, 2006, from www.familiesandwork.org/sparking/pdf/oklahoma_eval_report_final.pdf

Chase, R., Arnold, J., Schauben, L., & Shardlow, B. (2006). *Family, friend and neighbor caregivers: Results of the 2004 Minnesota statewide household child care survey.* St. Paul, MN: Wilder Research. Retrieved November 3, 2006, from http://edocs.dhs.state.mn.us/lfserver/Legacy/DHS-4516-ENG

Collins, A., & Watson, E. (1969). *The day care neighbor service.* Portland, OR: Tri-County Community Council.

Gordon, J. (2000). How our field participates in undermining quality in child care. *Young Children, 55,* 31–34.

Maher, E. J., & Kelly, J. F. (2007, March). Implementing and evaluating a pilot program for low-income grandmothers to support infant and toddler development. In E. J. Maher (Chair), *Creating an evidence-base of program models to support children in family, friend, and neighbor care.* Symposium conducted at the biennial meeting of the Society for Research in Child Development, Boston.

Musick, J., & Stott, F. (2000). Paraprofessionals revisited and reconsidered. In J. P. Shonkoff & S. J. Meisels (Eds.), *Handbook of early childhood intervention* (2nd ed., pp. 439–453). New York: Cambridge University Press.

Ocampo-Schlesinger, S., & McCarty, V. (2005). The Arizona kith and kin project. In R. Rice (Ed.), *Perspectives on family, friend and neighbor child care: Research, programs and policy. Occasional paper series* (pp. 22–25). New York: Bank Street College.

O'Donnell, N. S., Cochran, M., Lekies, K., Diehl, D., Morrissey, T. W., Ashley, N., et al. (2006). *Sparking Connections, Phase II: A multi-site evaluation of community-based strategies to support family, friend and neighbor caregivers of children. Part 1: Lessons learned and recommendations.* New York: Families and Work Institute.

Olds, D. L., Robinson, J., O'Brien, R., Luckey, D. W., Pettitt, L. M., Henderson, C. T., et al. (2002). Home visiting by paraprofessionals and by nurses: A randomized, controlled trial. *Pediatrics, 110*, 486–496.

Organizational Research Services. (2005, July). Family, friend and neighbor caregiver resource network – King County. SOAR Opportunity Fund/Sparking Connections evaluation report. Seattle, WA: Author.

Paulsell, D., Mekos, D., Del Grosso, P., Banghart, P., & Nogales, R. (2006). *The Enhanced Home Visiting Pilot Project: How Early Head Start programs are reaching out to kith and kin caregivers.* Final interim report submitted to the U.S. Department of Health and Human Services, Administration of Children, Youth and Families, Head Start Bureau. Princeton, NJ: Mathematica Policy Research.

Porter, T., & Kearns, S. M. (2005). *Supporting family, friend and neighbor caregivers: Findings from a survey of state policies.* New York: Institute for a Child Care Continuum, Bank Street College of Education.

Porter, T., Rice, R., & Mabon, S. (2003). *Doting on kids: Understanding quality in kith and kin child care.* New York: Institute for a Child Care Continuum, Bank Street College of Education.

Powell, D. R. (2006). Families and early childhood interventions. In W. Damon & R. M. Lerner (Series Eds.) & K. A. Renninger & I. E. Sigel (Vol. Eds.), *Handbook of child psychology: Vol. 4. Child psychology in practice* (6th ed., pp. 548–591). Hoboken, NJ: Wiley.

Rosenkoetter, S. E., & Knapp-Philo, J. (2006). *Learning to read the world: Language and literacy in the first three years.* Washington, DC: ZERO TO THREE.

Runkle, P. (2006, November). *Promising practices for family, friend and neighbor child care.* Panel presentation at the annual meeting of the National Alliance for Family, Friend and Neighbor Child Care, Atlanta, GA.

Steinke, P. (2006, November). *Promising practices for family, friend and neighbor child care.* Panel presentation at the annual meeting of the National Alliance for Family, Friend and Neighbor Child Care, Atlanta, GA.

Welch, N. (2002). *The staying power of kith and kin.* Tempe, AZ: The Insight Group.

Chapter 5

Lessons From Four Diverse Communities

One Saturday morning on a cold winter day in Minnesota, a group of 12 women gathered in a meeting room at a community center to talk about their work in caring for very young children. Nine women were caring for grandchildren, and three women were caring for children of close friends or relatives. The women attended the meeting in response to a letter of invitation from the meeting organizer, a child care expert at a child care resource and referral (CCR&R) agency interested in launching a project to provide support for informal caregivers. The participants described their caregiving arrangements (e.g., from 1 to 9 children at different times) and why they do the work (e.g., "to help my daughter"). They generated a list of topics they'd like to learn more about. Infant–toddler development, early literacy, special needs, CPR, first aid, sudden infant death syndrome, and communicating with parents were quickly identified as some of the areas of shared interest. The listing of topics moved to a discussion of joys and frustrations in caring for other people's children. There was talk of difficulties in setting limits with the children's parents, getting strongly attached to the children, finding time each day for taking care of one's self, and differences between rearing grandchildren and their own children. Several cried. The participants agreed to meet twice a month on Saturday mornings, shared contact information so they could communicate between meetings, and wanted to know if they could invite others.

This gathering occurred in one of four projects aimed at supporting family, friend, and neighbor (FFN) caregivers. The projects were initiated by the Archibald Bush Foundation of St. Paul, Minnesota, for the purpose of learning how to share information about the development and care of infants and toddlers with informal child care providers. Questions about program development and implementation strategies were at the forefront of the Bush initiative: How do programs and their host agencies prepare to work with the relatively unfamiliar population of FFN caregivers? What are effective ways to find and engage informal providers? What methods are useful in responding to the needs and interests of FFN providers?

This chapter summarizes lessons of the Bush initiative's efforts to find, engage, and support FFN caregivers. The chapter devotes a section to each of the three questions posed above and concludes with implications for future directions in strengthening the early childhood field's capacity to support informal caregivers. A full report of the initiative is available at the Bush Foundation's Web site (www.bushfoundation.org).

The projects were charged with developing a program of information and support to FFN caregivers in their community. The projects were to be small in scale and short term in duration, with no expectation of sustaining the developed program. The emphasis was on generating information about outreach strategies, including thoughtful reflection on what worked and did not work well. Trial and error was an acceptable way to proceed. To this end, the projects were called *learning* projects. Experiences and lessons across the four projects were to be shared among the projects frequently (see below) and eventually with the early childhood community. The Bush initiative occurred about the same time as the Early Head Start Enhanced Home Visiting Pilot Project and the Sparking Connections initiatives described earlier in this volume.

Although detailed procedures were not prescribed to the projects, the initiative provided three parameters. First, projects were encouraged to employ a community-based approach to developing a program of information and support *with* (vs. *for*) informal caregivers. Table 5.1 outlines key principles of a community orientation in contrast to a conventional approach dominated by professional perspectives. This was a working document throughout the period of the initiative, as described later in

Table 5.1: Contrasting Approaches to Program Development in Supporting Family, Friends, and Neighbor Caregivers

Program Feature	Conventional Approach	Community-Based Approach
Main question	What needs or problems have you seen in the informal providers or the children they care for?	How can we support you in the important job you are doing with young children?
Key informant	Other professionals	Caregivers
View of caregiver	Has deficits	Has both resources and needs
Recruitment	Print (e.g., fliers, letters, posters)	Personal (e.g., word of mouth)
Helping process	Professional gives to caregiver	Professional adds to insights and resources shared by caregivers
Source of key words to describe program	Professional perspectives and terminology (e.g., training)	Caregivers' perspectives and language (e.g., "get together")
Methods of providing support	Modeling, newsletters, presentations	Determined with caregivers
Number of support strategies	Usually one dominant approach	Several
Focus of growth	Caregiver	Both professional and caregiver
Sponsoring agency role	Extend existing knowledge and skill base	Learn or refine new ways to provide information and support

this chapter. The intent was to ensure that projects incorporated the views and experiences of informal caregivers in generating a project design. Second, the projects were to work with individuals caring for at least one child 3 years old or younger for 10 or more hours per week in an informal (unlicensed) arrangement. Lastly, project staff—coordinators and their supervisors—were to document their efforts by maintaining daily journals of their project-related actions and reflections on the work. They also participated in periodic interviews with Bush consultants responsible for providing technical assistance to the initiative (see below). Agencies were selected for developing a project through a grant proposal review process that began with agency submission of a letter of intent. Prior to inviting eligible agencies to submit a full proposal, Bush Foundation staff convened a meeting with representatives of interested agencies for the purpose of describing the planned parameters of the initiative. Population diversity was among the considerations in the Bush Foundation's decision-making process.

The projects received three types of support during the 18-month duration of the initiative. Bush consultants in early childhood organized and implemented four 1-day meetings of project coordinators and their supervisors for purposes of sharing current knowledge about supporting FFN providers and, importantly, facilitating discussion among project staff about their plans and experiences. These meetings were initiated with an orientation session prior to the beginning of project work. A focus of the orientation was the presentation and discussion of Bush Foundation-prepared summaries of available research on FFN caregivers and 11 state or local projects aimed at supporting the quality of FFN care through training or technical assistance. The 11 featured projects were identified in consultation with Bank Street College's Institute for a Child Care Continuum. One of the recurring features of each follow-up meeting was joint effort, through group discussion, to refine key elements of the community-based approach to program development as set forth in Table 5.1. Leaders of Bank Street College's Institute for a Child Care Continuum provided a 3-day training based on the curriculum described in chapter 3. Finally, a Bush consultant provided technical assistance and advice to each project coordinator. The frequency of these consultations varied across projects. Each project was encouraged to devote the first 3 months of the grant period to project planning, particularly in collaboration with pertinent leaders and members of the target community.

Below are brief descriptions of the four projects, their communities, and the caregivers they served[1]. Most providers cared for one or two children through an informal arrangement, although providers in the inner-city neighborhood project cared for an average of four children across various times of the day. Most providers cared for a preschool- or school-age child or children in addition to one or more children less than 3 years old. Across the four projects, about one half of the participants had been FFN providers for between 1 and 5 years. The suburban community project served a sizeable number of women who had been FFN providers for less than 1 year (45%), whereas the inner-city neighborhood project served many FFN providers with 6 years or more years of experience (50%). The number of program sessions with caregivers, in the form of group meetings or home visits, ranged from 7 to 10.

- **Inner-city neighborhood:** A CCR&R agency with a long history of training child care providers developed and implemented one of the projects for informal caregivers in an urban neighborhood with a substantial number of lower income and ethnically/racially diverse residents. A group method was employed. More than two thirds of participants were African American and 17% were Native American. A majority of caregivers were relatives of the child or children in their care (58%); others were friends/neighbors (25%) or cared for a mix of relatives' and friends' children (17%). One third had completed high school, and most others had some post-secondary education (42%) or college degree (17%). The project coordinator was an early childhood professional with experiences in a special project for recipients of welfare and in facilitating support groups.

---

[1] Information on caregiver characteristics is based on the following numbers of participants who completed demographic questionnaires: 12 in the inner-city neighborhood project; 15 in the project serving urban Somali immigrants; and 28 in the suburban project (8 of whom were enrolled in the parenting education group serving Somali immigrant women). Demographic information was not secured from participants in the project serving a tribal community.

- **Urban Somali neighborhood:** An agency that provides training and technical assistance to early childhood personnel developed a project for women in an urban neighborhood comprised primarily of recent immigrants from Somalia. Most of the women lived in two adjacent apartment complexes. The project used a group format, with meetings held in a meeting room in one of the apartment complexes or at the agency's nearby offices (transportation was provided). All participants in the project were Somalian, most of whom had recently relocated to the United States. Most cared informally for children of friends or neighbors (53%); others cared for children of relatives (47%). The project coordinator was a recent immigrant from Somalia with extensive professional experiences and credentials as a community health worker.

- **Suburban community:** The project serving a large suburban county was based at an agency that provided child care resource and referral services plus a family support program for at-risk children. The project worked with Somali women, all recent immigrants to the United States, through a collaborative arrangement with a parenting education program in which the women were participating. One half of the women were informally caring for one or more children of relatives, and the other one half were caring for neighbors' children. The project also served a different set of informal caregivers through occasional consultation work, usually via telephone calls initiated by the providers. The latter group was mostly European American (80%) with college degrees (55%), primarily caring for children of friends or neighbors (55%) or serving as a nanny (15%). The project prepared and distributed a newsletter for FFN providers. Three staff persons assumed responsibility for different geographic areas of the county. One staff member had experiences in child care referral work, another was a seasoned early childhood professional with a background in training infant–toddler caregivers, and the third staff member had child care center teaching experiences. In this chapter, the terms suburban Somali and urban Somali are used to distinguish the two Somali groups reached in the initiative.

- **Native American reservation:** The project was developed by early childhood staff affiliated with an infant–toddler caregiver training program based at a tribal college. The project was targeted to informal caregivers living on the tribe's reservation. The project provided home visits focused on early literacy and language development plus periodic group meetings. It also prepared and distributed a newsletter for the target population. This project ended several months early because of the departure of the project coordinator for another professional position on the reservation. The project coordinator was a teacher (licensed in early childhood and elementary education) with experiences in teaching infant–toddler development at the college level.

Preparing to Work With FFN Caregivers

The process of developing a new project for an unfamiliar population of caregivers was a significant challenge to existing agency practices and staff competencies.

Agency staff and project leaders often were outside their comfort zones in launching a new support program for FFN providers. The challenges included the following:

- Policies and practices that view licensure as the best method for improving child care quality;
- Limited linkages to FFN providers;
- Few experiences in developing a new program (vs. implementing a prescribed model); and
- A dominant history of "clients-come-to-us" approaches to training child care providers.

Over time, each project made good progress in addressing barriers to supporting informal child care arrangements. Progress was faster and on stronger footing when agencies hired project coordinators with extensive community outreach experiences and when agency executives provided leadership in encouraging broad-based agency recognition of FFN arrangements as a legitimate, valuable form of child care.

It appeared that each staff person needed time to discover through direct experience some core ideas about supporting FFN providers. The orientation and training sessions conducted with all project staff were rated by project coordinators as helpful in providing concrete tools for moving forward. These sessions did not fully "jump start" the projects, however. For instance, one coordinator announced at a meeting of all coordinators, "I've figured out that some FFN providers don't think of themselves as caregivers," even though this point was emphasized some months earlier in an orientation meeting. Too, informal child care was not a foreign world to the project coordinators—each coordinator had used one or more informal arrangements for her own child and one coordinator regularly cared for a grandchild on weekends—but initially each communicated uncertainty about characteristics of the target population. Becoming comfortable and knowledgeable about the diverse array of informal child care arrangements seemed to require time and increased contact with a range of FFN providers.

Generating a project name and description of informal caregivers underscored the limits of the FFN vocabulary.

The range of names used to describe FFN caregivers (see chapter 1) can lead to a practical problem in developing a program of support: What label best communicates the population of interest? The Bush initiative used the "kith and kin" terminology that, until recently, was a common reference to informal caregivers. Several projects did not find this to be a useful term, however. For instance, the project on a reservation initially called itself the "Kith and Kin Project" but abandoned the title when it became clear that few people understood its meaning. As the coordinator of one of the other projects stated at the beginning of the initiative, "If I don't understand what 'kith and kin' means, will the child care providers? There is so much jargon in the child care field. My first order of business is to find a different title for the work." More recently, project staff have indicated that the "family, friend, and neighbor" label, currently dominant in the field, also lacks clarity.

Project leaders fondly referred to the process of identifying a project title as the "name this child" task. A sizeable portion of an early meeting of project leaders was devoted to discussion of issues in selecting a name. Meeting participants quickly agreed that projects would avoid potentially off-putting technical terms such as "unlicensed" and "unregulated." There was less agreement on whether and how to communicate a focus on infants and toddlers, and a good deal of uncertainty about words that define FFN providers in ways that are understandable to lay audiences, including FFN providers themselves.

The names eventually generated by each project varied in emphasis. One project adopted the name "Caring From the Heart" in an effort to convey what the project viewed as a central dimension of FFN caregiving. Another project used the name "Friends and Family Program," whereas another emphasized infants and toddlers ("Infant Toddler Caregiver Resource Project"). Consistent with one of the principles of a community-based approach to program development (see Table 5.1), the administrator of the agency implementing the project for urban Somali caregivers invited two gentlemen in the Somali community to generate artwork for the project's brochure (the final drawing was of two Somali women sitting on a traditional chair used to nurse infants). The administrator also helped secure a person to translate the brochure copy into Somali language.

At the root of struggles in generating a project name is the lack of widely understood terminology for describing the role and functions of informal caregivers. Reactions to projects' descriptions of FFN caregivers are illustrative of the problem. A newspaper article about the project in the tribal community described the effort as "a service for friends and family who babysit for a child or children who are 3 years old or younger." The "babysitter" label annoyed one provider. She called the project coordinator in response to the article, indicating that she "doesn't just babysit...I care for the children." In another instance, a project coordinator contacted a prospective participant via telephone at the suggestion of a coworker. The coordinator was not certain the individual was still providing informal care, so the coordinator asked the person if she "did child care." The response was "no." The coordinator then asked, "Do you babysit?" Her response: "Well, you could call it that. What I really do is watch my grandkids."

Some licensed child care providers communicated negative reactions to a project targeted to FFN caregivers.

Staff in two of the four projects, both operated by CCR&R agencies, received negative feedback about an initiative aimed exclusively at FFN caregivers.

In one of the agencies, members of an advisory committee responsible for recommending financial allocations for training participation incentives expressed considerable concern about the merits of supporting FFN caregivers, including the provision of incentives. The committee was comprised of center directors, licensed family child care providers, and other child care professionals. Committee members indicated that their own programs were suffering from low enrollments, leading to staff layoffs in some centers, and communicated the belief that extra support should be given to licensed providers rather than unlicensed caregivers. Ultimately the committee approved the request for training incentives, though it did so with reservations. "I was shocked," the FFN project coordinator communicated the day after the meeting. The coordinator also perceived a lack of enthusiasm among other staff in the agency during the early phases of work with FFN providers.

In the other agency that received some resistance to offering an FFN effort, the project sent letters to licensed and unlicensed providers on the host agency's provider lists (the unlicensed providers had received a child care subsidy), inviting unlicensed providers to participate in a focus group discussion about a new project focused on FFN child care. Licensed providers were included in this mailing with the expectation that they might know unlicensed providers who would like to participate. The letter asked for a telephone reply. Most of the providers who called in response to the letter were currently licensed providers who wanted to know if they could participate in the focus group and join the project. When the project coordinator responded by emphasizing the project's specific interest in FFN caregivers, some licensed providers expressed disappointment that "there isn't anything like this for us— why is this just for the unlicensed providers?" The project coordinator found several of the licensed providers to be particularly angry that the project was limited to FFN caregivers. "My heart went out to these women," the coordinator wrote in her journal about the calls. "These licensed providers were putting in all of the requirements to remain licensed; they wanted this type of support as well."

Finding and Engaging FFN Caregivers

The projects mostly found FFN providers with an existing connection to a formal support system for their caregiver role.

Each project initially identified prospective participants who were already linked to an established program focused on the care of young children. Most prospective participants were not receiving ongoing training and technical assistance for their informal caregiver role, however. Some participants had previously enrolled in child care training workshops or programs. This was especially the case with providers in the inner-city neighborhood project. Prior to participating in the Bush Foundation project, two thirds of participants in the inner-city neighborhood project had received child care training, ranging from 12 to 44 hours.

It was common for projects to find prospective participants through lists of legally unlicensed providers participating in a child care subsidy program as well as lists of self-identified unlicensed providers who had participated in one or more child care trainings such as a workshop. One project coordinator gave a presentation about the project to participants in a provider licensing training session in anticipation that some participants may not qualify for or receive a license.

In addition to contacting FFN caregivers on child care subsidy program and training lists, the project serving the suburban community found informal caregivers through a partnership with a parenting education program that conducted a weekly group session with Somali women. At one of the parenting group meetings, participants expressed interest in learning more about child care. Eventually many of the women in the parenting group disclosed that they were informal caregivers. This led the parenting program to arrange for the FFN support project to take responsibility for alternate sessions with this particular group.

Contact with "known" prospective participants sometimes led to "unknown" informal providers via word of mouth. This pattern occurred in the project serving urban Somali women, where subsidized FFN providers introduced the project coordinator to friends or acquaintances who were FFN caregivers not receiving a child care subsidy (see below). The project serving an inner-city neighborhood also found FFN caregivers by word of mouth, through friends who attended the first group meeting, and through visibility at the community center where the project's group meetings were held (e.g., the receptionist regularly provided care for a friend's child on weekends).

Agency lists of unlicensed providers were not always an efficient, guaranteed path to FFN caregivers.

There were striking differences across the projects in whether contact with unlicensed providers identified through child care agency lists led to project participation. One project sent an invitation to a project orientation meeting to approximately 150 unlicensed providers who had received a child care subsidy administered by the agency or identified themselves as a legally unlicensed provider in registering for a child care training offered by the agency. The letter was accompanied by a stick of gum, enclosed as an attention-getting device. Twenty-five of the some 150 individuals who received the letter responded with an intention to attend the first meeting, and 12 of the 25 individuals attended the first meeting (described in the first paragraph of this chapter). The coordinator of the project serving urban Somali women was able to conduct a home visit with nearly all of the individuals on a list of current recipients of a child care subsidy for FFN providers.

In contrast, a third project encountered problems in conducting a telephone and mail survey with prospective participants by using agency lists of (a) unlicensed provider participants in the child care subsidy program, (b) persons expressing interest in providing child care, and (c) unlicensed providers who had attended child care trainings. One problem was that the registration form for participants in agency trainings did not include a category for FFN caregivers. There were categories for child care center staff, licensed family child care providers, and "other." Calls to individuals who marked "other" revealed that most were assistants in licensed family child care homes. Another difficulty was that only the agency list of FFN providers currently receiving a child care subsidy was up to date. For instance, only 3 persons were reached in telephone calls to more than 40 individuals on one list (none of the 3 was interested in the project or currently providing care). Many telephone numbers had been disconnected. In a subsequent telephone survey with a different list of approximately 130 individuals, the project coordinator was able to speak with 40 individuals during the first round of calls. Nine of the 40 persons met the criteria for participation in the project (providing FFN care to one or more children less than 3 years old for 10 hours per week). Others were no longer providing care or provided care to older children. (Four of the 9 eligible participants expressed interest in project participation.)

A fourth project also found, through telephone calls to individuals on lists of child care providers secured through a job training program, that many individuals were no longer providing care or had a disconnected telephone line. In several instances, individuals responded negatively to the telephone call, wanting to know how their name and telephone number had been secured and asking that they not be contacted again.

Difficult-to-reach FFN providers were most readily found through families.

Projects used several different outreach efforts to identify FFN care-givers who were "unknown" to the projects—that is, not on available lists of child care subsidy recipients, child care training participants, or existing programs such as the suburban parenting education group described above. This more invisible set of informal caregivers may have needs and interests that differ from those of informal caregivers who have found their way to subsidy programs and other forms of formal assistance such as a parenting program.

The project serving a tribal community found some of its participants through tribal college students who were parents. The project coordinator visited classes and approached students in campus gathering places (e.g., cafeteria) to ask if students had a child care arrangement with a relative or friend. Those who responded "yes" were told about the project and asked for permission to contact the relative or friend. Most of the informal providers identified through this method were not on lists of child care providers secured through other agencies. The project coordinator found that when she contacted providers via telephone, they were more receptive to talking with her than providers she identified through agency lists. About one quarter of FFN caregivers identified through the college students enrolled in the project.

Projects also pursued print-based outreach efforts and personal contact with prospective participants via young children's programs at local libraries. The limited yield of these efforts is described next.

Print-based community outreach generally was not successful in identifying FFN caregivers.

The use of print to publicize a new program is a common approach to promoting awareness of a community issue and an agency's response. This method helps introduce a new program to other agencies and professionals in a community, and provides yet one more reminder of a program's existence to individuals who have learned of the program through other means. Two of the projects initially attempted to identify caregivers primarily through print-based outreach strategies in their target communities. The efforts were not productive. For example, as one of several outreach strategies, the suburban project placed fliers announcing the availability of a support program for FFN caregivers in numerous community locations, including supermarkets, apartment buildings, a mobile home park, and a family resource center. The postings prompted telephone calls from several individuals, one of whom wanted financial assistance to enroll in a CPR refresher course. A brief description of the project also was placed in the Sunday bulletins of at least five churches. It seems that this effort produced no inquiries. The project serving a Native American reservation also put posters describing the project in numerous community locations. The posters generated no telephone calls or other forms of contact with the project. A newspaper article about the project did prompt a response, as indicated earlier.

In addition to the impersonal nature of print-based outreach, one-way communications are not helpful in addressing the previously discussed challenge of describing FFN caregivers. In a personal exchange, project staff can try out a variety of descriptors, read nonverbal cues, and respond to questions in an effort to effectively communicate the scope and intent of the project. Print communications offer few options for conveying key words, particularly when there is uncertainty about what key words will be meaningful.

Not surprisingly, personal contact—eventually used by all of the projects— proved to be superior to impersonal means of connecting with FFN caregivers. However, personal contact was not uniformly effective, as described next.

Not all personal contact is the same. The quality of a project's personal exchanges with FFN caregivers seemed to influence decisions about project participation.

Some forms of personal contact were more useful than others. The most productive in-person exchanges with prospective participants generally permitted some focused discussion of the project. Specifically, it appeared beneficial for the setting of the exchange to be relatively free of distractions and for adequate time to be available for the project worker to provide a clear description of the project and to talk with the caregiver about her or his interests.

The project serving urban Somali women is illustrative of the conditions noted above. The coordinator identified FFN caregivers in the target neighborhood through agency lists of individuals receiving child care subsidies. She made the initial contact by mail and then a follow-up telephone call, when phones were available, aimed at scheduling a home visit. She also met prospective participants during visits to the apartment buildings where most providers resided or provided care. Word of mouth was a highly productive means of finding FFN care-givers in this Somali neighborhood once some initial contacts with caregivers were established. For example, on one of her first home visits, the coordinator met with 4 women who were informally providing care to infants and toddlers. The caregiver who originally was the sole focus of the home visit invited 3 other FFN caregivers to join the session. Each brought the child or children in their care. The coordinator described the FFN support project in some detail and led a discussion of the caregivers' experiences with the caregiver role by asking a series of questions (see next lesson). She also gave each woman a scarf, a highly valued item of cultural significance that could be used multiple ways (e.g., privacy shield for breastfeeding, protection from wind). Nearly all prospective project participants contacted in this manner became active members of the FFN support project. Existing ties among the caregivers may have been an influential form of peer support for project participation.

Contrast this effort with a creative yet time-consuming form of personal contact with FFN caregivers in the suburban project. As one means of recruiting FFN caregivers, project staff participated in preschool story hours at local libraries. The project's presence at local libraries was usually an add-on to the library's regular story hour during which the project staff person would offer an activity for infants and toddlers as a follow-up to a book reading conducted by the children's librarian. Typically these activities focused on sensory-motor experiences or music and movement. The project staff person used the children's interactions with objects as an opportunity to talk with adults about some aspect of early development and to describe the project's interest in supporting informal providers. The project provided snacks and juice. Sometimes the project staff person would assume responsibility for the entire story hour.

Generally at each library session the project worker was able to connect with one or two FFN caregivers providing care for an infant or toddler. The project worker found that the story hour sessions provided suffi-cient time for discussion of the project when a relatively small number of children participated (under 10) and when adults were able to divide their attention between their child or children and the project worker. Often there was a larger number of persons in attendance, however, which led to significantly reduced time for focused discussion of the FFN support project. Under this condition, discussion with prospective participants generally occurred at the end of the story time when indi-viduals were preparing to depart and often dealing with tired or highly active children. The pattern was for individuals to attempt to politely listen to the project coordinator but seldom engage in extended discus-sion. Also, in settings with larger attendance it was challenging for the project coordinator to efficiently identify the informal caregivers.

In addition to the time constraints noted above, the project coordinator's role in the story time may have inadvertently created some confusion about how the FFN support project offerings would differ from what is available at the library story time. None of the informal caregivers iden-tified through the library story sessions attended more than one group event for FFN caregivers sponsored by the project, although some did participate occasionally in individual consultations with the project

coordinator through telephone calls and/or home visits. This was relatively infrequent and intermittent.

**Methods for learning about FFN providers' interests were an integral
part of engaging prospective program participants.**

The important task of learning about the interests of prospective program
participants was a core element of outreach to FFN providers. Information
gathering and recruitment were merged functions. Information gathering
from prospective participants focused primarily on their content interests, not their preferred methods of project participation (e.g., group
sessions vs. home visit). Some examples are described below.

Discussions during the home visits to informal caregivers in the
urban Somali neighborhood (described above) were guided by a
12-item questionnaire the project coordinator developed with agency
colleagues. Some questions were common to a generic needs assessment (e.g., preferred time and place of project gatherings), but other
questions were specific to the population. One novel question that
consistently generated a good deal of discussion with caregivers simply
asked, "What's the challenge of caring for children here in the U.S.
rather than at home?"

The project serving the tribal community generated and distributed a
newsletter with information about the care of infants and toddlers to
prospective program participants, identified primarily from lists of
unlicensed providers receiving a child care subsidy. Focus groups of
prospective participants were subsequently convened. As part of the
discussion at group meetings, informal providers described what they
found useful in the newsletters and what other types of information
they would like to receive. An advantage of this arrangement is that
providers were responding to concrete rather than abstract possibilities
for program support of their caregiver role.

The inner-city neighborhood project had its first in-person contact with
prospective participants at a group meeting convened by the project for
purposes of learning providers' interests and describing parameters of
the project. Prospective participants were identified through lists of
informal providers receiving a child care subsidy. The invitation was

extended via a letter. The session essentially became the first meeting of an ongoing information and support group (see next section). Attendees discussed their interests, agreed on a meeting schedule, and shared basic information about their caregiver work.

Two projects also attempted to learn the interests of informal caregivers by distributing surveys that were to be returned via U.S. mail. This was not a productive approach. Response rates were low, and some respondents did not complete all items.

Responding to Caregivers' Interests and Needs

Different methods of supporting caregivers—home visits, group meetings, newsletters, providing child care equipment and materials—were equally well received.

The literacy-focused home visits with informal caregivers on the reservation, the group sessions in urban and suburban communities, the child care materials and equipment provided by all projects, and the newsletters developed and distributed by two of the projects were well received by participants. We do not have information on whether some prospective participants declined participation in a project because a different service delivery method was preferred. None of the group-based projects offered a home visiting option. Providing home visits and group meetings as a combined delivery method was not successful on the reservation. Caregivers participated in the home visits but rarely attended the periodic group meetings. This pattern has been found elsewhere (see chapter 4).

Across the four projects, participants expressed appreciation for a program that "says we're important." Recognition of the contributions of FFN caregivers to the growth and development of infants and toddlers was consistently identified by project participants as a valued feature of each project. Providers in the project serving the suburban community, for example, found the "Caring From the Heart" program title to accurately represent their approach to caregiving.

The opportunity to connect with peers was cited by participants in the group-based inner-city neighborhood project as a major benefit of involvement. Participants indicated that they valued the opportunity to find and form ties with other informal caregivers. Peer discussion of common interests appeared to be as worthwhile to participants as the child care information provided by the project (e.g., "I get a lot of support from the other providers and I like the issues we discuss."). The peer support component of the two group-based projects serving Somali populations may have been less salient because the women had ties with one another that predated the project.

Food was a regular feature of group sessions across all projects. Provisions ranged from snacks and refreshments to full-fledged meals prepared by the project coordinator using culturally appropriate recipes.

The safety items and child care materials provided by each project reportedly were put to good use. Reports of home visits conducted to recruit informal caregivers in the urban Somali neighborhood (see above) and in the tribal community indicated that some homes were void of routine safety provisions for infants and toddlers (e.g., no security gates on stairways) as well as manipulative objects. The children's books provided by the project serving the reservation were especially novel.

Projects differed in how equipment and materials were distributed. One project used items as incentives for project participation. Points earned by caregivers for attending sessions could be "exchanged" for child care items of interest to each participant. Another project placed project-selected toys for infants and toddlers on a table at each group session, and caregivers selected items in an equitable manner agreed on among themselves. The project did not impose rules or expectations about ownership of the items, and the project coordinator privately wondered if the items would remain with the child or the caregiver.

Most of the information shared with project participants was an adaptation of existing child care training resources.

With the exception of the project serving the reservation, the projects used existing child care training resources for conducting sessions with participants. It was common for guest experts rather than the project coordinators to make presentations at group sessions (e.g., a nutrition expert presented a session on feeding infants and toddlers, a nurse presented a session on sudden infant death syndrome, a bilingual fire-fighter conducted CPR training). Accordingly, in the three group-based projects, coordinators typically functioned as organizers of sessions (e.g., securing outside speakers) and less frequently as a primary source of expert information presented at a meeting. Interpreters were provided for the two groups serving Somali women.

Project coordinators found it helpful to provide guest experts with infor-mation about participants' interests and circumstances in advance of a presentation. For example, presenters were urged to avoid technical terms and to not assume that the caregivers wished to become licensed child care providers. Care also was taken in the selection of guest pre-senters. For the CPR training conducted in the project serving urban Somali women, the coordinator secured a firefighter with established relationships with child care providers in the city's East African com-munity. He has a reputation for respectful patience in training sessions, willingly repeating information that participants initially find to be confusing. Project coordinators tended to lead sessions for which there was no known curriculum resource (e.g., communicating with parents who are relatives or close friends).

The project serving the reservation worked with students enrolled in a child development associate's degree program at the tribal college to generate activity packets for distribution and use at home visits. Each of the activity packets focused on a theme related to a children's book and included toys (e.g., stacking rings) and materials to support the use of songs and a manipulative (e.g., recipe for play dough). The books were secured through corporate donations solicited by the project. The project coordinator was wary of using an existing curriculum, believing that materials developed on the reservation and for the reservation would be more credible with prospective users.

The infant–toddler focus was both a strength and a limitation.

In general, caregiver participants in each project welcomed the opportu-nity to learn more about the care of infants and toddlers. Information on infant temperaments seemed to be of greatest interest, partly because this topic was new to most participants. Many caregivers who participated in the project also cared for preschool- and school-age children, and often expressed stronger interest in learning more about the care of older children than in children less than 3 years old. Also, some prospective participants contacted by project staff did not care for infants and toddlers and communicated disappointment that a program of support was not available for informal caregivers of older children. The infant–toddler content boundaries of the projects seemed artificial in these instances, and led some project coordinators to believe that a multiage approach would be more responsive to the realities of family child care arrangements.

For immigrant populations, the projects served as cultural mediators.

In both the urban and suburban projects serving Somali women, group sessions typically addressed cultural differences in the care of young children. The women communicated pride and confidence in their child-rearing abilities. As one caregiver told a project coordinator, at an early age "our mothers taught us everything we will need for the future: cooking, cleaning, care for children, administration of the family and our traditional way of doing everything...and we helped our mothers care for the children, so when you grow up you already know how to take care of children." Nonetheless, the caregivers expressed feelings of isolation and uncertainty in caring for young children in the United States. They were puzzled by immunization practices (e.g., one caregiver described how breast milk and goat's milk were sufficient protection against diseases in her native land). They expressed many concerns about the children's safety and confinement to indoor spaces. They were accustomed to children being outside for most of the day, but viewed Minnesota weather as either too hot or too cold and the neighborhood's outdoor spaces as unsafe (e.g., worried about kidnapping). They thought the apartments were too small for children to spend their entire day.

Cultural differences in food were explored with considerable interest. Prepared and packaged foods in the United States were a particular curiosity (e.g., one caregiver described how camel milk, camel meat, and local crops were the nutritional mainstay in her rural Somalia). In the project serving the urban Somali group, for example, a session with a nutritionist ran well over the allotted time because participants had many, many questions and issues to discuss. In the suburban Somali group, a session that included an introduction to snacks commonly used with young children in the United States generated strong, negative reactions to "ants on a log" (which is typically celery stick, peanut butter, and raisins).

The content focus of the urban project serving Somali immigrants extended beyond child care issues. The project coordinator made arrangements for classes for English language learners to be held at a community center in the neighborhood where project participants resided. The project also helped several caregivers attend a nanny training program by providing interpretation services and, near the end of the project, helped two participants take steps to become licensed child care providers. The project coordinator received calls daily for assistance in making clinic appointments and in understanding and completing forms, including child care subsidy requests. She provided transportation to training sessions not held in the caregivers' neighborhood. She followed up with caregivers who did not attend training as anticipated (e.g., in one instance a schedule had been read incorrectly). Importantly, the coordinator, who was a recent immigrant herself, served as a role model for the caregivers regarding the process of becoming familiar with a new country. In a meeting with two caregivers interested in becoming licensed, for example, she showed a book on English grammar that she was studying herself and told where she had purchased the book.

Project participants differed widely in their goals and stability in the informal caregiver role.

Some participants were desirous of becoming licensed child care providers or credentialed to serve as an aide in a public school. This varied across projects. For example, about one third of participants in the inner-city project wished to pursue licensure at the conclusion of the project. Nearly all of the Somali women sought to enroll in a training program that led to a preschool aide credential. Child care licensing was out of reach for most of these women because their apartments did not meet licensing requirements. Other participants were happy with their current informal caregiver status, sometimes because the arrangement was viewed as temporary and other future work paths were of interest.

Some participants were in and out of the informal caregiver role during the period of contact with the project. In the project on the reservation, for example, about one third of participants stopped providing care while enrolled in the project. Typically they did not wish to participate in the project (i.e., receive a home visit) once they were no longer providing informal care, sometimes indicating they were uncertain whether they would provide child care in the future.

Project work contributed to changes in staff competencies and agency practices.

None of the projects fully implemented a community-based approach to program development as described in Table 5.1. Yet important progress was made on several fronts, particularly in understandings of informal care arrangements. An unintended outcome of the Bush Foundation initiative is that staff and agencies were better equipped to responsively serve FFN populations at the end compared to the beginning of their project. Consider the following examples. Several project coordinators became members of a state-level planning committee organized by a state agency to consider ways of strengthening supports to FFN providers. A child development expert who made a guest presentation at one of the FFN group sessions noted on a follow-up survey that "my biggest realization was that these women take their responsibilities seriously and are proud of the work they are doing. They are also hungry for information that will help them give quality care to children." One of the agencies added questions about child care arrangements to its routine intake procedures for a family support program. The supervisor of a project in another agency noted the effort had "stirred the waters ... related to our organization's intent to serve legally unlicensed providers more fully."

Future Directions for Capacity Building

The experiences across the projects described in this chapter reflect some unique differences, probably based in part on staffing and community factors. At the same time, there are striking similarities in the experiences of the four projects.

What are key points of departure for future efforts to strengthen the capacity of the early childhood field to support FFN caregivers? The lessons of the projects described in this chapter, combined with the experiences of other initiatives summarized in prior sections of this volume, suggest the directions identified below.

- **Finding FFN caregivers:** Strategies for finding informal caregivers who are not already connected to an existing system of support for child care providers such as a child care subsidy program are needed. Identifying FFN providers through families is one promising approach that needs further exploration. Family support programs may be an appropriate organizational platform for this type of outreach.

- **Differentiated support systems:** As training programs and researchers "unpack" the population of FFN providers, it is becoming clear that one size of support does not fit all caregivers. For some providers described in this chapter, project participation served as an "on ramp" to licensure training. Yet other providers had absolutely no interest in formalizing their role. Future work should consider efficient ways of enabling this self-sorting process to occur early in the engagement process, so providers can be matched to appropriate resources. For example, FFN providers who wish to become licensed may be better served in a training program aimed at individuals seeking a license.

- **Organizational readiness:** To date, the literature on how to support FFN providers comes mostly from agencies that intentionally choose to promote quality in informal child care arrangements. Yet even these organizations, presumably high in motivation to work with FFN caregivers, encounter initial barriers in realizing their goals with FFN providers. We do not know how to help organizations that are *mandated* to work with FFN caregivers respond to the challenges of finding and supporting informal providers. More generally, the field needs information on specific steps that agency leaders can pursue to equip their organizations for effectively engaging informal providers.

- **Training and support resources:** Curriculum and related resources are needed for addressing dimensions of infant–toddler care that are unique to informal arrangements, particularly the complexities of relations with families (see chapter 2 for a list). Also, guidelines for ensuring continuity and coherence of content across training sessions may benefit programs that tend to use different guest speakers.

- **Staff preparation:** In addition to curriculum resources, the field needs training tools that enable staff to work effectively with informal providers. Experiences of the projects described in this chapter indicate that responsibility for supporting FFN providers should be assigned to seasoned staff members, especially those who have community outreach experiences and, ideally, some familiarity with the target population. Still, additional support is likely needed. An identification of competencies of effective supporters of informal child care providers would be an important step in this direction.

- **Intensity of support:** We need information from in-depth evaluations of training and support programs on what level of intensity is likely to yield significant improvements in the quality of care and in outcomes for children. Research on family child care training programs (e.g., Kontos, Howes, & Galinsky, 1996) may provide useful benchmarks for examining program dosage effects.

The origin of the Bush Foundation's learning projects may offer some insight into a requisite step toward improved support systems for informal child care arrangements. The initiative was an outgrowth of a long-standing Bush Foundation grant-making program designed to improve the quality of infant–toddler development through caregiver training (www.bushfoundation.org/publications/inftodfullrpt.pdf). Organizers of the training were highly successful in reaching providers in licensed facilities but consistently encountered difficulties in connecting with caregivers in informal arrangements. As a result, the substantial number of babies and toddlers in informal settings was not being touched by the trainings. This led the Bush Foundation to renew its commitment to promoting the well-being of babies and toddlers "wherever they are" and to contribute to the field's understanding of how to effectively engage FFN caregivers. The critical "aha" moment involved recognition of (a) the numerous limits of existing systems for supporting adults who care for young children and (b) the need to approach FFN caregivers on their own terms. Serious progress in strengthening the early childhood field's capacity to ensure high quality in *all* infant–toddler care environments may require a similarly simple yet potent "aha."

Reference

Kontos, S., Howes, C., & Galinsky, E. (1996). Does training make a difference to quality in family child care? *Early Childhood Research Quarterly, 11*, 427–445.

About the Author

Douglas R. Powell, PhD, is a Distinguished Professor in the Department of Child Development and Family Studies at Purdue University in West Lafayette, Indiana. His research focuses on the development and effects of programs to support adults in caregiving and teaching roles with young children. Currently Dr. Powell directs a large-scale study of professional development with prekindergarten teachers regarding early literacy and language development, supported by grants from the federal Institute of Education Sciences. He also has directed major studies of the effects of educational support programs for parents of children birth to 3 years old. He is a consulting editor for *Child Development*, a member of the editorial board of *Parenting: Science and Practice*, and former editor of the *Early Childhood Research Quarterly*. This ZERO TO THREE volume is based on Dr. Powell's work as a consultant to the Archibald Bush Foundation in St. Paul, Minnesota.